Persian Rose

FARAHNAZ AMIRSOLEYMANI

FARI PUBLISHING

LONDON | NEW YORK

FARI PUBLISHING

Published by Fari Publishing

Printed in the United States of America.
Published simultaneously in United Kingdom, and Canada.

Library of Congress Control Number: 2018908170

ISBN 978-0-692-16247-7

FIRST EDITION

Typography: Cochin, Gothic

PUBLISHER'S NOTE
The advice contained herein is for informational purposes only.
This book is not a substitute for psychological treatment, or for
medical care by a physician. The author and the publisher disclaim
any and all liability for any consequences, damages, and
outcomes (including property damage, physical injury, or death)
that may occur as resulting from the use of the information
contained in this book.

For More Information Visit:
WWW.FARIPUBLISHING.COM
WWW.FARAHNAZAMIRSOLEYMANI.COM

5

Contents:

Introduction 8

The Persian Diet (Unani) 10

Chapter 1: Persian Holidays & Customs 14

Chapter 2: Persian Flavor 24

Chapter 3: A Persian Rose 36

Chapter 4: Small Plates (Mezzehs) 42

Chapter 5: Bread (Nan) 57

Chapter 6: Soups (Ash) 66

Chapter 7: Stews (Khoreshts) 76

Chapter 8: Persian Rice (Polo) 90

Chapter 9: Main Dishes (Khoraks, Kabobs, & Koofthes) 105

Chapter 10: Preserves & Fragmented Foods (Moraba & Torshi) 120

Chapter 11: Hot & Cold Beverages (Nooshabeh) 130

Chapter 12: Desserts (Shirini) 142

Index 155

Persian Rose

A Persian Rose by any other name...
Growing up I was always told to be a Persian Rose. A Persian Rose is a woman with grace and poise. Whose presence can warm the room like the sun, with eyes sparkling, and a charitable heart. A rose has an undeniable natural charm, a dazzling smile, and has impeccable manners. She is sensuality personified with a mysterious demeanor that makes her magnetic. People are drawn to her like bees to honey; she leaves a positive lasting impression on everyone she encounters. She isn't afraid to live in the moment and just be herself. However, she is not perfect; she takes risks, and learns from her mistakes. A Persian Rose is intelligent and driven, she creates beauty through whatever she does. A Persian Rose is unique and possesses a quality that is truly serendipitous.

A Persian Rose above all else knows the value of family, and takes great pride in preparing luxurious simple healthy meals for her loved ones.

A Persian Rose is a treasure and is within us all...

Persian Cuisine is quite distinct from other Middle Eastern food, emphasizing on enticing dishes full of elegance, and flavor: saffro aromatic herbs, orange blossom water and rose petals, succulent pomegranates, all make for an array of tantalizing recipes which makes Persian cuisine truly unique. Persian food is a refection of the ancient Persians who were lovers of poetry and the arts. Inher ent: in the rice cooked to fluffy perfect are the words of Rumi, and the chai (tea) that was savored by the legendary king's of Persia's past. Iran's (Persia) rich history, culture, and geography has greatl shaped Persian food. Historically, Persian culture is vast with a wid array of indigenous people with traditions, customs, and languag of their own. With this said, many of the dish's in this book reflect the cookery styles from Northern Iran in the provinces of Tabriz ar Mazandaran, wear my family hails from.

Persian cuisine is unpretentious, authentic and cooked with love. Full of unexpected flavors surrounded by exotic spices, while presenting a dazzling tapestry of colors (much like a fine Persian rug), a delight for all the senses. Focused on the freshest ingredients from the lush, fertile areas of the Caspian Sea, to the deserts of the Persian Gulf.

Persian food features a healthy combination of a wide verity of products that include: yogurt, fruits, vegetables, meats, fish, rice, and herbs. That creates bold, delectable, luscious, savory dishes with rice being the main attraction.

To make Persian food more accessible, I have carefully tested and measured every recipe, to ensure the accuracy of the dish (you won't have to worry about a pinch of this or that!) this will give you the confidence to prepare Persian food with easy-to-make perfection.

In this book, I'm thrilled to share my passion for cooking along wi generations worth of family recipes that are truly priceless jewels. addition an introduction to Persian holidays & customs, and secre to cooking like a Persian rose.
I'm delighted to invite you into the celebration of love, life, cultur and delicious food. As we say in Persian, Noush-e Jan!

The Persian diet:
unani

Ayurveda is an ancient practice of alternative medicine native to India. The first mentions of Ayurveda are made in Indian medicinal literature written around 1700 BCE. The main goal of Ayurvedic medicine is to restore health and increase longevity through the establishment of balance. Thus, practitioners of Ayurvedic medicine see imbalance as the main cause of all physical and psychological ailments. In order to treat this imbalance, practitioners of Ayurvedic medicine turn mainly to plant-based medicines and treatments that are the building blocks of the Ayurvedic diet.

Of course, it is not surprising that this form of alternative medicine spread quickly throughout the ancient world and helped influence and advance the medicinal practices of many ancient civilizations. For example, a close look at ancient Chinese medicine reveals the heavy influence of Ayurvedic medicinal practices on this form of ancient medicine. The ancient Chinese philosophy regarding the Yin and Yan nature of foods is in direct correlation to the Ayurvedic diet's emphasize on the medicinal balancing nature of certain foods. Furthermore, it's hard not to correlate the Ayurvedic notions of Vata, Pitta and Kapha with the notions of spirit, water and blood which work together to balance the flow of Qi.

Though the intricacies of Ayurvedic medicine and ancient Chinese medicine are well known throughout the western world, the heavy influence of the Ayurvedic diet and medicine upon the cuisine and medicinal practices of the ancient Persian culture is still one that requires further exploration. Like the Chinese, the Persians drew heavily upon the Ayurvedic notion of balance when fashioning their cultural cuisine and medicinal views. However, unlike the ancient Chinese whose medicinal practices advanced in the direction of the Meridian theory of pressure points and flows of energy, the Ancient Persian's medicinal practices advanced in the art of "Ishoku Dogen" which means, "Food is medicine and medicine is food".

In keeping with the philosophy of "Ishoku Dogen" the Persian food culture evolved to treat food as a source of disease prevention. In keeping with the Ayurvedic principles, the early Persian physicians, and philosophers such as: Hakim Ibn Sina (also know as Avicenna) developed an intricate system (Unani) of combining foods based on the categorizations of four humors: cold, hot, dry, and moist. The description 'hot' or 'cold' doesn't relate to the temperature of food but rather to the effect - food has on the body.

All food is broken down by enzymes in the stomach: consequently this effects the bodies cells and ultimately how the body functions. Enzymes react to the 'hot' and 'cold' food. For example, a 'cold' food like an orange slows down the digestive process, which in turn slows the body down. On the other hand, 'hot' foods like spices speeds up the digestive process, and increases the bodies metabolic rate.

A persons diet is also determined by season, and where they live and the climate. This is where the humors 'dry' and 'moist' come to play. So if someone lives in a dry area they need to consume moist foods, and if you live in a moist environment you need dry foods – in means of keeping balance. Also according to Unani practices people must also eat seasonally – meaning buying local organic ingredients (farm to table), and buying food seasonally (natural harvest time).

This system of food combination was designed to help maintain balance within the body and thus ward off various physical and mental ailments brought on by imbalance within the body's natural flow.

This ancient philosophy of combining foods based on their categorization of Unani is an integral part of Persian culture and is still currently being practiced. However, what sets Unani apart from the Ayurvedic diet developed in India is the fact that the Unani diet includes both white and red meats, as well as other animal products, into its categorization. This is not surprising, given the fact that the Persian diet is a semi-vegetarian diet, with close ties to the Mediterranean diet. As follows is a list of 'hot' and 'cold' foods. Please note: this book is vegetarian. However, I categorized meats on their 'hot' and 'cold' properties for knowledge bases only.

garmi

(Hot Foods)

Apples, bananas, carrots, caviar, chicken, chickpeas, dried fruits (all), eggs, figs, garlic, herbs (except parsley & coriander), lamb, nuts (all sorts), olives, onions, quince, radishes, rosewater, spices (except sumac), vinegar, wheat, honey.

sardi

(Cold Foods)

All unripe fruit, all fresh fruit (except apples, quince, figs, & bananas), all vegetables (except carrots, radish, okra, onions, garlic, red & green peppers), beef, coffee, dairy products, lentils, rice, sugar, sumac, verjuice.

bi taraf

(Neutral Foods)

Feta, and tea.

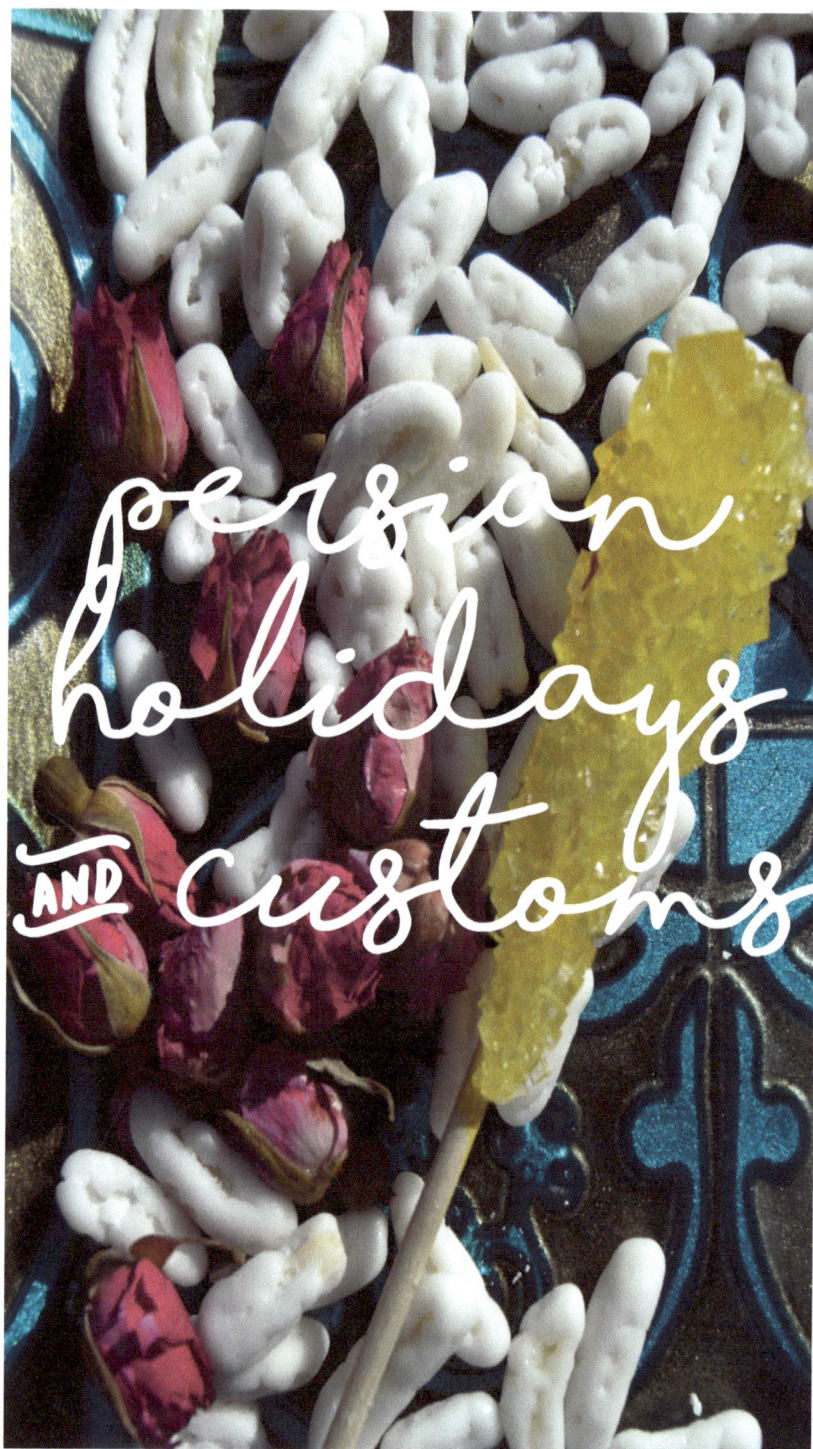

persian holidays and customs

Red Wednesday Festival (Chahar Shanbeh Suri)

Chahar shabeh suri falls on the last Wednesday of the year, one week prior to the new years (Nowruz). Chahar Shanbeh Suri is based on the belief that there is darkness in the world before there was light. The festivities start in the early evening with children and adults dressing in costumes and banging on pots and pans with a spoon, which is called Gashog-Zani, while walking from door to door asking for treats, a custom similar to trick-or treating. Later that evening the main event takes place jumping the fire. It is customary that seven little fires are lit consisting of dried bushes and shrubs, which are placed on the ground. Adults and children gather and jump over the flames while singing "Sorkhi-e to az man. Zardi-e man az to." Meaning, your fiery red color is mine and my sickly yellow paleness is yours. Loosely translated, this means you want the fire to take away all the bad, and replenish you with good luck. Later that same night, some adults participate in falgoosh (Fortune-hearing) a ritual where a person will make a wish, and stand at the corner of an intersection, or hide behind walls to listen to conversation of those passing by - in means of trying to interpret the statements or the subject of the passers-by as an answer to one's wish.

The Persian New Years (Nowruz)

Nowruz, which means "new day" is the celebration of the Persian New Years. It has been said that on this day the legendary King Jamshid Shah was crowned. Nowruz is celebrated on the first day of spring and is determined according with the spring equinox and coincides with March 21, or the previous/following day. Nowruz is the celebration of life and new begging's, and is deeply rooted in Zoroastrianism. The preparation for Nowruz begins several weeks prior to the spring equinox. Some of the most widespread Nowruz customs are:

Khaneh Tekani (spring cleaning): before Nowruz every room in the house most be thoroughly cleaned from carpets, to curtains, it is even customary to repaint walls with a fresh coat of paint. In addition, it is also traditional for everyone in the family to buy new clothes for Nowruz.

Sabzeh (sprouts): It is customary to plant wheat or lentils in a small pot, the growing sprouts proclaim the coming of Nowruz.

Sofreh-ye Haft Seen:

The haft seen is the center of Nowruz consisting of a table covered with a fine tablecloth, and decorated with seven items starting with the Farsi letter "Sin" ("s" in English). The seven items stand for the seven angelic heralds of life: renewal, health, happiness, prosperity, joy, patience and beauty. Each item on the Haft Seen symbolizes one of the heralds. As follows is a list of the seven items:

Sabzeh (Sprouts): represents renewal and growth.

Sir (Garlic): represents healing, and good health,

Senjed (a sweet fruit): represents love and passion.

Somagh (dried Sumac): represents the color of sunrise, symbolizing the spice of life.

Serkeh (vinegar): represents patience.

Sib (apple): represents health and beauty, and is the season's first fruit.

Sekkeh (coins): represents prosperity and fortune.

In addition, the ceremonial display includes a mirror to reflect life, goldfish in a bowl of water to signify life, a copy of the family's holy book (Qur'an, Avesta, Torah, etc…) to sanctify the table, sweets (shirini), and flowers. There are also colored eggs painted with great care normally by children and symbolizes fertility. The last item that is placed on the haft seen are candles, which represent the light of life.

Sal Tahvil (New Years Eve):

Sal Tahvil or the Sa'at-e Tahvil is New Year's Eve, which is the official time for the Spring equinox. Sa'at- tahvil is an important moment, as it is a time for forgiveness and putting aside petty differences. As the countdown begins for Nowruz the entire family gathers around the haft seen, in their new clothes celebrating and exchanging Nowruz greetings such as "Nowruz Mobarak" meaning Happy New Years, and "Sad Saal be in Saal-ha (whishing you 100 more Happy New Years)". At this point it is customary for the elder of the family to give gifts to the children, and the family continue to celebrate by drinking tea and indulging in sweets. It is also believed that the first visitor sets the tone of the New Year, so generally the most innocent member of the family - usually a child is sent to go outside, then nock on the door and therefor becomes the first visitor for the New Year.

16

Haji Firooz, Amoo Nowruz & Naneh Sarma:

With Nowruz comes Haji Firooz a mythical character dressed in an elaborate red costume, with a face painted in black. Haji Firooz ushers in the Nowruz with song, and dance while tapping a tambourine to bring joy for the New Year. Ammo Nowruz (Uncle New Years), a wise elder brings gifts to children on Sal Tahvil (New Year's Eve) much like Santa Claus. Ammo Nowruz in Persian folklore is said to makes the wishes of children come true, and ensures that they are happy. It is also tradition to hear the story of Naneh Sarma (Lady of the cold spells) who is the symbol of winter and is in love with Amoo Nowruz.

Deed-o Bazdeed (New Years Visits):

The New Year's celebration continues for twelve days, and it is customary to go from house to house visiting family and friends. It is customary for the young to start their visits with the elder first, bring sweeties, flowers and paying their respects. During these visit's it is a celebration of love and happiness rejoicing in the New Year. It is customary for guest to indulge in sweets, tea, fruits and a lavish feast. While Children receive "eidi" gifts such as money and toys.

Sizdah Bedar (The Day 13 Outing)

Sizdah Bedar is the last day of Nowruz and is a day filled with relaxation and fun outdoors. Sizdah means 13 and Bedar means away or out. Persians consider the number 13 unlucky so for this reason on the 13th day of Nowruz is spent outside the home. Sizdah Bedar is celebrated by going to a garden, park, or any land that is covered with greenery and blossoms in means of avoiding evil and bad sprits. Once at the garden it is customary that the sabzeh (sprouts) be thrown in a river or stream. It is believed that the sprouts absorbed all the negativity of the last year, and once placed in the river, the river will wash away all the negativity for a blessed New Year. The day is spent listening to music, dancing, play games, and eating traditional foods to bring good luck for the New Year.

The Rain Festival (Jashn-e Tirgan).

Jashn-e Tirgan is an ancient Persian festival celebrated in July (Tir) the fourth month of the Persian calendar. This festival is based on Persian mythology. Legend says that two leaders Iran and Turan were at war and fighting over land. In order to resolve the War they agreed to have Arash-e Kamangir shoot an arrow, and wherever the arrow landed that would create the new border between the two kingdoms. It is said that archangel Tir, or Tishtar (lightning bolt) appeared in the sky generating thunder and lightning which called forth the rain to celebrate the joyous occasion of peace between the two kingdoms. Today, some Persian of Zoroastrian religion celebrate this day by throwing water in the air, and at each other, while dancing, singing, and reciting poetry. The customary dish served is spinach soup.

Autumn Festival (Jashn-e Mehregan):

Jashn-e Mehregan is the festival of the autumn harvest and takes place in the Persian month Mehr (ninth or tenth day of October) and is dedicated to the Goddess of light Mithra. Jashn-e Mehrgan originated as a festival offering thanks to the Mithra for the abundance of fresh produce that farmers gathered during the autumn harvest. Today the festival is also associated with love and friendship as Mithra is associated with knowledge, love, light and friendship. There are many different renditions of how and why Mehregan has come about. However, in modern days Mehregan is a festival for all religions and marks the welcoming of the new season. During Mehregan family and friends gather together to enjoy each other's company. The celebration ends with bonfires and fireworks celebrating the new season.

*Zoroastrianism celebrate by creating a sofreh (table covered with a tablecloth) decorated with dry wild marjoram. A copy of Khordeh Avesta (Little Avesta), a mirror and a sormeh dan (an antimony container) along with sweets, rosewater, flowers, fruits and vegetables, and nuts. Silver coins and lotus seeds are placed in a small bowl of water scented with marjoram extract. Frankincense (kondor/loban) are burned at the sofreh along with Syrian rue seeds (espand). At noon the family stands in front of the sofreh to pray. After chilled fruit drinks are served, and antimony is rubbed around the eyes. While handfuls of marjoram, lotus and sugar plum seeds are thrown over each other's heads while they embrace one another.

The Winter Feast (Shab-e Yalda)

Persians celebrate Shab-e Yalda on the longest night of the year, which falls around December 21st. Shab-e Yalda is the celebration of the rebirth of the sun, this festival represents that there is always light at the end of the tunnel (meaning good always prevails). On this night, family and friends gather around a Korsi (heater), or fireplace for a large feast and enjoy a variety of fresh fruits that will be going out of season. On Shab-e Yalda it is tradition to stay up all night celebrating until the sun comes out in the morning.

The Fire Festival (Jashn-e Sadeh)

Jashn-e Sadeh is the festival of the discovery of fire, and the defeat of darkness. Jashn-e Sadeh marks a hundred days of winter, and is celebrated on January 31st of the year. There are many suggestions as to the origins of the fire festival. Some say the festival comes from the legend of Shah (king) Hushang, the first shah of the mythological Kayanian dynasty. It is said Hushang was climbing a mountain, when he encountered a black snake coming towards him, in his defense Hushang threw a rock at the snake and missed. Instead, the rock hit another large rock, causing sparks to fly, which started a fire. Fire broke out in a brilliant splendor, and burnt the snake. Hushang was filed with cheer and praised God for revealing to him the secret of lighting fire.

Today, Jashn-e Sadeh is celebrated by Persians of all faiths, in means of keeping ancient Persian culture alive. On Jashn-e Sadeh Friends and family gather firewood, and build a large bonfire at sunset. Traditionally people sing and dance around the fire, while throwing frankincense (kondor) in the fire to ward off evil. Chestnuts, potatoes and nuts are roasted in the fire and enjoyed by all.

Day of Love (Sepandarmazgan)

Sepandarmazgan is the celebration day of love, affection, and earth. Sepandarmazgan dates back to the 20th century BC. Celebrated on the 29th of Bahman in the Persian calendar, which corresponds to February 18th. The Zoroastrian tradition is named after Spenta Aramiti the goddess of devotion and unconditional love, who is the spiritual mother of all, and symbolizes passion, friendship and modesty. On this day, women and girls are held in the highest regard and garnished with lavish gifts of flowers, jewelry and sweets by the men in their life. This custom reminds men to honor and respect women on this day.

19

Persian weddings are lavish beautiful unions that consist of many different traditions. A Persian wedding consist of two parts the Aghd (religious ceremony), and the Aroosi (wedding party).

The aghd is the legal ceremony for a Persian wedding and is usually filled with joy, music, and singing. During this ceremony, a sofreh aghd (the wedding spread) is prepared for the bride and groom. The spread is typically set on the floor facing the east so that the couple will face the light. Each item of the sofreh aghd has its own decorative and symbolic meaning, all of which help to bring a fruitful marriage. At this point, the officiant arrives and proceeds to read the agreed upon vows and begins the ceremony. After the preliminary blessings and a few words about the importance of the institution of marriage, the officiant asks the groom if he wishes to enter the marriage contract. Then the bride is asked the same question. Here, the bride traditionally plays shy and makes the groom wait for her hand in marriage by not answering the question right away. The guests scream in the background, "the bride has gone to pick some flowers" or "the bride has gone to bring rose-water". She then says yes on the third time and the couple are pronounced husband and wife, a kiss and the exchanging of rings ensues. As the ceremony is being performed, married female relatives of the couple hold over the couple head a white silky Ghand (cloth). While two Kalleh Ghand (crystallized sugar cones) are rubbed together, showering the couple with white powder. This act symbolizes the sweetness of life. In addition, a small part of the ghand cloth is sewn together using colored silk threads and a needle, symbolizing sewing the mother-in-law's or "nay-sayers" lips together. Then the couple and the witness sign the official documents, and the couple are pronounced man and wife. The bride and groom exchange rings and kiss. At this point, the asal (honey) is presented to the happy couple. Here, the groom dips his pinky finger into the honey and gives some to his bride. She does the same in return (this act ensures a sweet and happy life together). The wedding guests indulge in the sweets that were represented at the sofeh (which are thought to be blessed and lucky). To finalize the ceremony the couple lights two candles that symbolize bring light to their new life together.

20

Jashne Aroosi

Jashne Aroosi (wedding party) is the reception and is a festive celebration filled with music, dancing, and feasting. The Aroosi is quite similar to a western-style wedding reception, which takes place after the agah. One special Jashne Aroosi tradition that seems to be a favorite of all is the Raghseh Chagoo (knife dance). The Knife dance begins with the bride and groom arriving at their cake, they will look for the cake knife and – will not be able find it. Only to see moments later that a female (family member or close friend) is dancing with the knife. The groom is to convince the dancer to hand over the knife, by giving money to the dancer. Once the dancer takes the money, the knife is passed on to the next dancer, and so on. A little back and forth, and a few dance moves later, the couple are finally given the knife and are able to cut the cake. After which more dancing and celebrating ensues until the early hours of the morning!

Asoos keshoon

Asoos keshoon (bring the bride) is when the bride and groom are escorted to their new home or hotel. Close family and friends follow the newlywed's in their cars till they meet their destination. It is customary for the family and friends to honk their horns through the streets in means of announcing the newlyweds. Traditionally this ceremony dates to Zoroastrian times. When the father of the bride and family & friends would walk the shy virgin bride to her new home (groom's house) in means of making her feel comfortable. Once at the house the bride's father receives the bride's welcoming fee from the groom's family.

Patkhati

Patkhati (by the bed) is a quick ceremony that takes place the day after the wedding in the afternoon. On this day female guests bring presents to the Bride in her new home, and the couple are officially considered married. It is customary in a Muslim household that the groom leaves during this ceremony. Small snacks and tea are served to the guests, while one of the bride's relatives opens the gifts, and announces the name of the person who had given the gift. After all the gift's have been open – the guest will usually pamper the bride by bringing her to the hair-salon to have her hair styled. When leaving the hair-salon the mother of the bride will call the groom, so he can welcome his beautiful bride when she arrives.

Pagosha

Pagosha takes place soon after the wedding. Close relatives and friends will invite the couple over for dinner. At this meal the newlyweds are introduced to society, this custom is meant to make the newlyweds feel comfortable as husband and wife.

Birth of a child

For Persians it is a blessing to have a child, and is the notion for marriage to be fruitful and procreate. In Persian culture children are gifts from god and a necessary component for a happy marriage. Generally, once a couple is married they are expected to have a child within the first year. When a woman becomes pregnant, she becomes the center of attention of everyone in the family. For those that believe in old Persian folklore once a woman has given birth it is customary not to leave her alone as she is weak and "Al" an evil spirit will eat her liver. In addition, the newly born baby is never left alone for the first 40 days, not even for a minute. On the eve of the sixth day (shabe shish) after the birth of the child, a small family party is held. This small party is the naming ceremony. An elder of the family or holy person has the honor of naming the baby. The baby is given two names, the name by which he or she is called and a religious name. Payers are whisper in the baby's ear followed by their two names. After the naming ceremony family and friends gather for dinner.

Nazri (Cooked in Honor of)

Nazri is a religious offering of food to the Imans, or god, in hopes of receiving something of higher value (such as a husband, or child). Once the person's wish has been granted, they most make a special food once a year on a religious day of their choice, and give this food to the needy. This offering may be an entire meal, or just a sweet like shole zad (saffron rice pudding). The food of Nazri is b lieved to have healing powers and brings good luck to those

Persian Hospitality (Mehman Hediyeh Kho-last)

Hospitality is the core of Persian culture. In Persian culture guests are thought as a blessing from god "Mehman hediyeh kodast". When a guest enters a Persian household they are treated as royalty, they are given the best seat in the house, the best food, and are the center of attention. It should also be noted that whenever a newcomer (guest) enters the room, all those present most stand up as a sign of respect, even if you know the person or not. If you are the newcomer (guest) entering the room, you may ask them to remain seated by saying: "befarmaid, khahesh mikonam" (please do stay seated).

Taarof (ritual politeness)

Ta'arof is a beautiful part of Persian culture that is deep rooted in Persian hospitality that represents being polite, gracious and humble. Ta'arof is a verbal dance between an offerer and the acceptor, that continues until either party agrees. It is customary for the acceptor not to accept the offer of the offerer until the third time.

Example of Ta'arof:
For example, a host (offerer) offers a guest a cup of tea. The acceptor (guest) politely refuses, even if they are very thirsty. The host will offer a cup of tea a second time, and the guest still politely refuses. Finally, on the third time the gest will accept the cup of tea.

Another example of a Ta'arof:
You are shopping at a store and you ask the price of a vase, the shopkeeper in return will say it is not worthy of you, and that the vase is free. The shopkeeper is being polite and hobble, after asking the shopkeeper the price severally more times he will give you the price.

For some the act of ta'arof is troublesome (a waste of time), and they will say "ta'arof Nakonid" which means to stop ta'arofing.

Behshkan (Persian Snap)

Behshkan is the traditional two-handed Persian finger snap, no one knows where it originated. However, the behshkan can be used to get a party started, while your dancing, or used in applause.
behshkan how to:
1. Place your hands together like a "prayer".
2. Slide your thumb from your dominant hand, & place behind back of other hand.
3. Place Fingers on the corresponding fingers.
4. To snap place index finger from dominant had on the corresponding index finger, and bring the dominant index finger to the middle. The
5. You can clamp your dominant thumb down to create a louder sound.

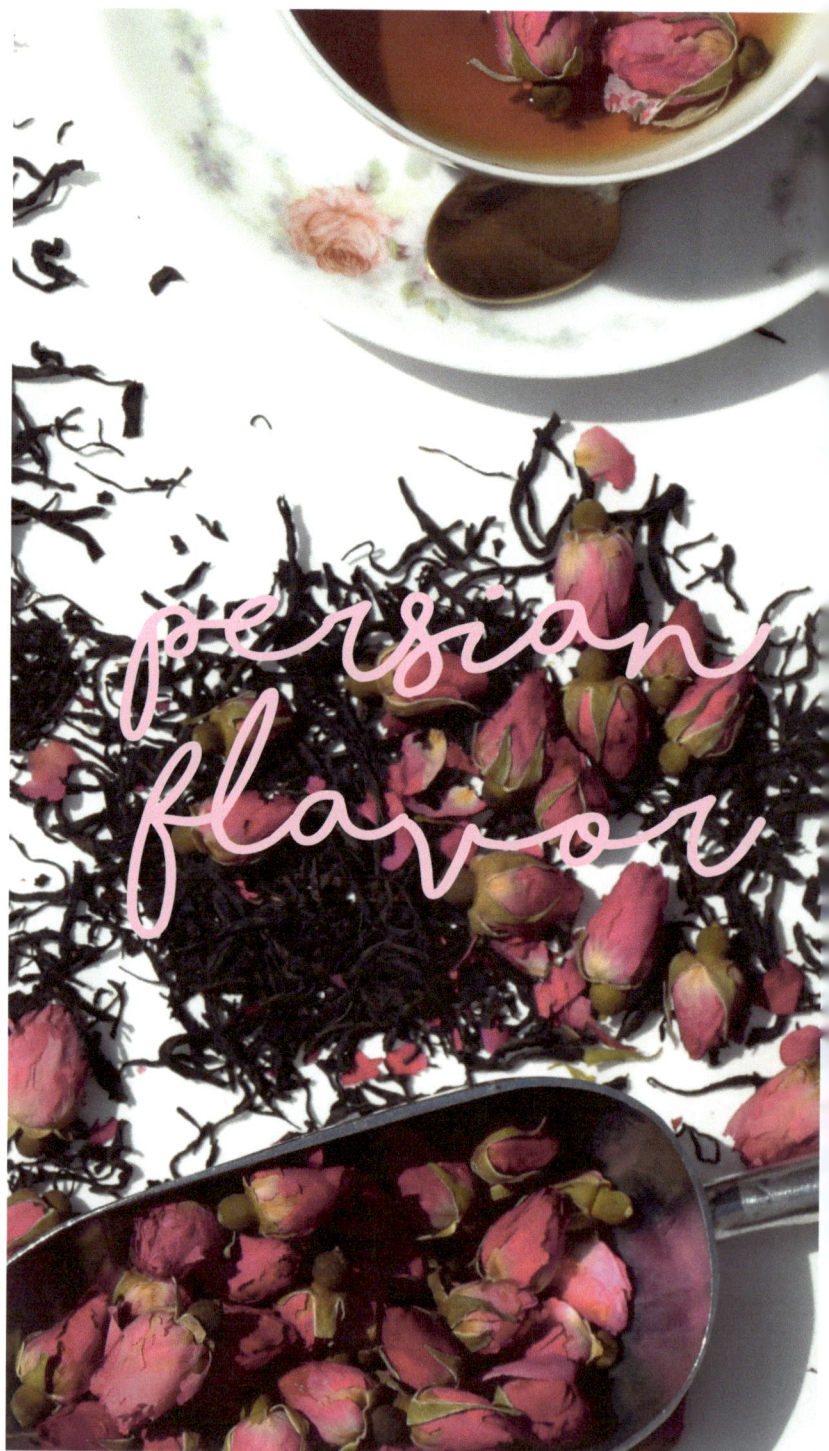

persian flavor

The key to cooking delectable Persian food is getting to know your ingredients: becoming familiar with the intended flavors, aromas and textures. Most Persian dishes are made with ingredients that you are probably familiar with, and some of the more exotic ingredients might require a trip to your local Persian or Middle Eastern grocer. At the end of this chapter you'll find three classic Persian spice blends.

*Please note: Most persian dishes have slightly different ways of being prepared according to region & preference. Please feel free to adjust recipes to your liking. Also most recipes in this book can be made vegetarian by simply omitting the meat.

legumes — beans, peas and lentils

Legumes are used very regularly in Persian cookery, and are an important source of protein, and iron. Legumes are an ideal addition for anyone's diet, and are a natural boost of energy. Legumes can be enjoyed fresh or dried. Chickpeas, lentils, red beans, and split peas are the most frequently used Legumes in Persian cooking.

Storage
Keep dried legumes stored in a cool, dry place, out of light, for up to 6 months.

Preparation
Before cooking, measure the amount of legumes needed for the recipe. Place legumes on a white plate and sort through the legumes, discarding shriveled or discolored beans, pebbles, and any other debris. Place legumes into a bowl of water let soak overnight (this reduces the cooking time, and removes the gas-promoting un-digestible carbohydrates). After soaking legumes, discard any legumes that float to the top, drain, and rinse. Use as directed in the recipe.

herbs

Fresh Herbs are used in a variety of Persian dishes. Herbs are so popular in a Persian household they are eaten raw (Sabzi khordan). The most commonly used herbs are basil (sweet), cilantro, fenugreek, mint, parsley (flat-leafed), spring onions, and tarragon

Sweet Basil (Reihan)
Basil native to Iran, has a mild flavor and a beautiful aroma, and is widely used. In Iran basil is stepped in the water – and drunk as tea for a remedy for nervous and digestive system problems.

Cilantro (Ghishniz)
Cilantro, also know as coriander. Is a tantalizing flavor, and has a number of medical uses. A natural ant-bacterial, and anti-inflammatory, that aids in digestion and is a natural mood booster. Rich in flavonoids that enhance the power of vitamin c, and prevent cells from oxygen damage. Cilantro is used in fresh and dried.

Fenugreek (Shambaleeleh)

Fenugreek is and aphrodisiac, and as my "bibi" (grandmother) says is used to make men happy wink… wink… Fenugreek is used fresh and dried, and is used in soups and stews, such as koresht-e ghormeh sabzi.

Mint (Nana)

Refreshing, cooling, calming… Mint is widely known as a natural breather freshener. Mint is rich in vitamins A, C, and b12. Mint is used in a variety of dishes, and is always accompanied by chai (tea).

Flat-leaf Parsley (Jafari)

Flat-leaf parsley the world's most popular herb and was once worn as crowns by the Greeks. Parsley is a used in many herb mixes in Persian cooking.

Spring onions (Piazche)

Spring onions are from the onion family and have a distinct onion-garlicky taste, and are best know as a cold remedy, that strengthens the immune system. In Persian cooking both the bulb and stems are used.

Tarragon (Tarkhun)

Tarragon a member of the daisy family, and has a very strong peppery flavor. In Iran tarragon is traditional given to children that are picky eaters to stimulating their appetite to ensure that they grow properly.

Fresh herbs can be kept for up to a week. The secret is to wash herbs quickly in cold water, pat dry, and cut of ½ inch of the bottom part of the stem. Place herbs in a glass of water (like flowers in a vase), and change water daily. Cover the top of the herbs with a lightly damped paper towel to lock in moisture, and keep herbs in the refrigerator.

fruits *and* vegetables

Persian Cucumbers (Khair)
Cool as a cucumber... Persian cucumbers, also know as a "mini seedless cumber," is dark, seedless, slender and has a subdued sweetness that is rather lovely.

Tomato (Gojeh Farangi)
Tomatos are widely used in Persian cooking fresh, and in paste form.

Eggplant (Badenjan)
Eggplants in Persian culture are called the "poor mans meat". However, eggplants are a staple food and are found in a wide range of dishes. There are several varieties of eggplants. I prefer the thin long eggplants, as they tend to be less bitter and work better with khoreshts (stews).

Lemon and Lime Juice (Ablimu)
Lemon and lime juice is used as an unexpected burst of tangy flavor to aashs (soups), khoreshts (stews) and salads. Citrus juice is high in vitamin C, and has amazing antibacterial properties, that help clear blemished skin.

Pomegranate (Anar)

Pomegranates are the symbol of fertility, and love in Persian mythology, and are a true jewel. Pomegranates are featured vastly in Persian cuisine. Pomegranates seeds are used as a garnish, and the juice is made into pomegranate molasses.

Barberries (Zereshk)

Barberries are tart bright red fruit that comes from a thorny shrub. High in vitamin C, barberries in Persian cooking are usually used dried, adding a unique tartness to any dish.

oils and nuts

Oil (Rohgan)

When it comes to oil, always use the best-quality extra virgin oil, as this has the most subdued flavor. I also recommend cooking with ghee when frying since it has a high smoke point. Store oil in a cool dark area. * Also please note all recipes can be adapted to your preferred cooking oil, such as: organic cold pressed coconut oil.

Pistachio Nuts (Peshet)

Pistachio nuts are marveled in Persian cooking for their delicate taste and bright green color. Pistachios are cholesterol free. Furthermore, Pistachios are packed with nutrients such as omega-s fatty acids, and rich in fiber. Use as a garnish or eaten as a snack.

fish, meat and dairy

Fish (Mahi)

Fish is eaten widely in the south of Iran by the Persian Gulf, and in the north by the Caspian Sea. When buying fish fillets check that the flesh is firm and that there is no ammonia smell, this is an important step to ensure freshness.

Meat (Gusht)

Lamb is the most popular meant in Persian cooking, but most recipes are interchangeable for beef or chicken. When purchasing meat always buy organic. Organic meat is Free of antibiotics, and added hormones that are dangers to your health.

Lamb (Barre)

When buying lamb always choose the youngest lamb available, the flesh should be a light rose color, and have pure white fat around the edges.

Beef (Gushtegav)

When buying beef, regardless of grade always buy beef with good marbling (flecks of fat). The more marbling in a piece of beef means the beef will be tender.

Chicken (Juje)

When buying chicken, the chicken should be practically odorless; if the chicken has an odor don't buy it.

Feta Cheese (Panir)

This tangy delicious Luxury is packed with calcium. I prefer to use French feta to Greek feta because its lower in sodium. If using Greek feta, soak feta in warm water for about 20 minutes to reduce the salt.

Yogurt (Mast)

Yogurt is used extensively in Persian food from fresh to sun-dried (Kashk). It is said yogurt is so popular in Persian cuisine because of Queen Poorandokht, who ruled Persia in 630–631 B.C., she was especially fond of yogurt, hence why yogurt is a major stable of Persian food.

rice ~ berenji

Rice (Berenji)

Rice is the foundation of Persian food, and a staple for all. Many Persians feel that they have not had a proper meal until they have eaten rice. Persian cookery has a variety of ways of preparing rice, which makes rice very versatile. Persian rice is mainly grown in northern Iran in the regions of Gilan and Mazandaran by the Caspian Sea.

The two most common types of Persian rice are domisah and sadri. However, Persian rice is not easy to obtain abroad, as an alternative I recommend basmati rice: as the texture, flavor and aroma are the nearest equivalent to Persian Rice.

Storage
Keep rice stored in a cool, dry place, in an airtight container.

Preparation
Before cooking, measure the amount of rice needed for the recipe. Place rice on a white plate and sort through the rice, discarding pebbles, and any other debris. Place rice into a bowl of water let soak for 2 hours (this reduces the cooking time, and removes excess starch). After soaking rice, drain, and rinse. Use as directed in the recipe.

rose water and rose petals
golab va gole-e sorkh

Persian cookery frequently uses rose water, and rose petals, to add a delicate luxurious flavor and aroma to many savory or sweet dishes. Rose petals also make a lovely garnish. When buying rose petals make sure you buy culinary petals, and not those that have been preserved for potpourri.

persian spice cabinet

dried herbs
Angelica (Gol-par)
Basil (Reyhan)
Cilantro (Gishnaz)
Fenugreek (shanballieh)
Mint (Na'na)
Persian lime powder (Gard-e Limu-Omani)
Persian limes, Whole Dehydrated (Limu-Omani)

spices
Cayenne pepper
Cardamon (Hel)
Cinnamon (Darchin)
Cloves (Mihkhak)
Cumin, Ground (Zierh)
Curry Powder (Kari)
Ginger (Zanjebil)
Nigella Seeds (Siah danseh)
Nutmeg (Jowz-e hendi)
Saffron (Za'feran)
Sumac (Somaq)
Turmeric (zardchubeh)
Vanilla (Vanil)

dried flowers
Rose Petals (Gloe-e sorkh)
Lavender (Ostokhodos)
Jasmine (Yas)

persian spice blends

persian kabob spice mix — advieh ye kabob

This is a wonderfully warming aromatic spice blend that you can use with any red meat.

Ingredients
4 tablespoons ground sumac
2 tablespoons ground onion
2 tablespoons powdered garlic
2 tablespoons ground turmeric
2 tablespoons dried cilantro
1 tablespoons ground ginger
1 teaspoon ground nutmeg
1 teaspoon ground clove

Method
Mix all ingredients thoroughly. Place in an airtight container and use when required.

persian stew spice mix ~ advieh ye khoresh

Advieh-ye khroresh is the base for most khoreshs (stews), and adds a delightful depth.

Ingredients
4 tablespoons ground coriander
4 tablespoons ground cinnamon
3 tablespoons ground cumin seeds
2 tablespoons ground cardamom seeds
2 tablespoons ground rose petals
1 teaspoon ground nutmeg
1 teaspoon ground clove

Method
Mix all ingredients thoroughly. Place in an airtight container and use when required.

persian rice spice mix ~ advieh ye polow

Advieh-ye Polow is available read-made at your local Persian grocer. Nevertheless, I prefer to make my own to ensure freshness.

Ingredients
4 tablespoons ground coriander
4 tablespoons ground cinnamon
4 tablespoons ground rose petals
3 tablespoons ground cardamom seeds
2 tablespoons ground cumin seeds
2 tablespoons ground Saffron
1 teaspoon ground nutmeg

Method
Mix all ingredients thoroughly. Place in an airtight container and use when required.

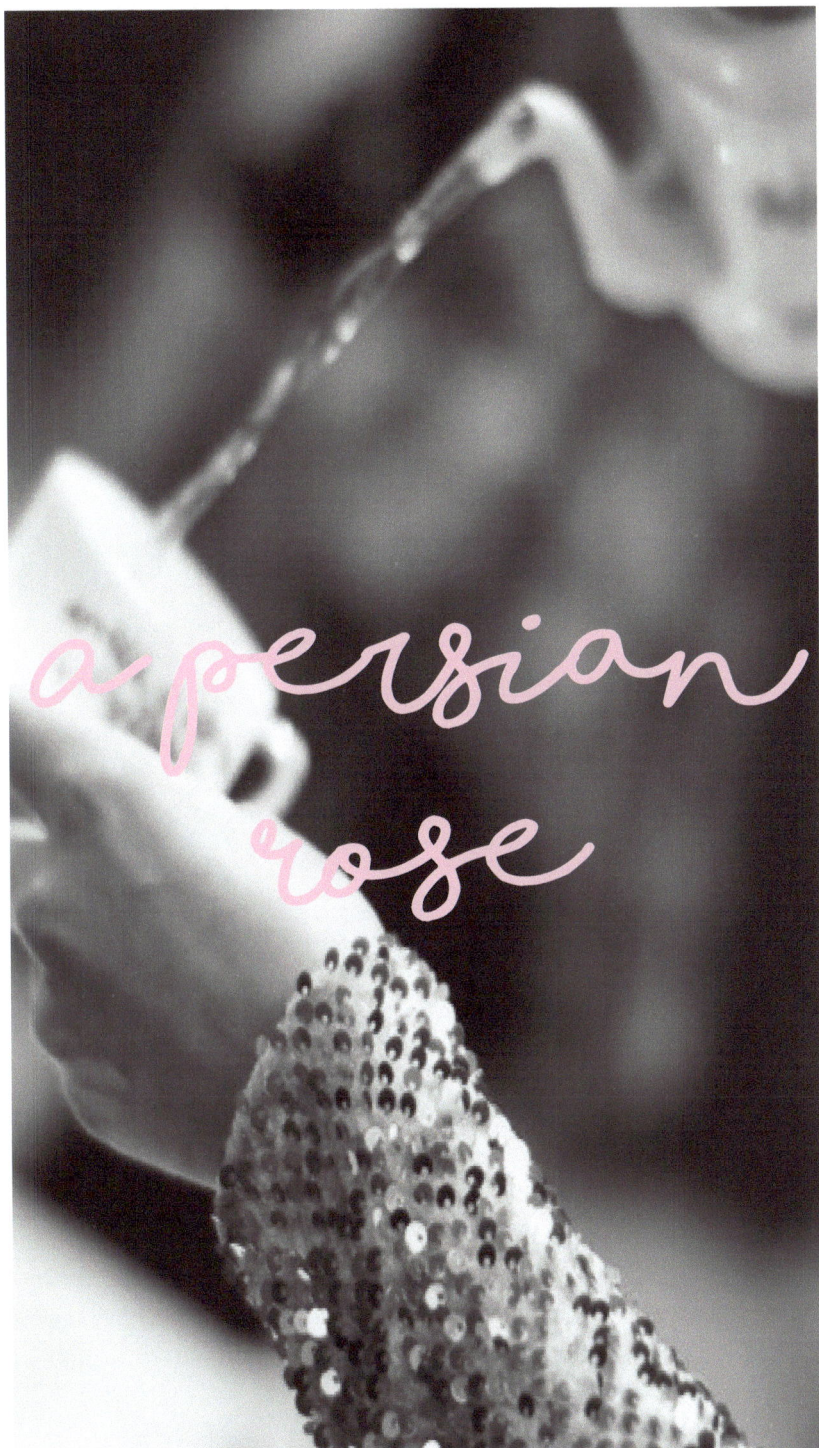

a persian rose

A Persian Rose is a housewife that knows all the secrets of Persian cooking. She's aware that preparing a delicious healthy meal enriches one's family. The time and delicate care put into every dish is a beautiful gift, and an expression of love. Details such as fresh baked bread, rice cooked to fluffy perfection - show we care. The traditions we create at a meal table affect the very nature of our family's, and play a major role in their memories. With this said, it is important to make each memory beautiful.

A meal can set the tone of a day, a year, and a life.

the secrets of a persian rose

Planning a Balanced Menu

Before cooking write down a menu with all the items you plan to serve. Make sure that the meal is balanced, and you have all the ingredients needed to prepare the meal. This simple step will ensure a meal peppered with ease.

Pre-Peppering A Meal

Most Persian dishes can be prepared a day in advance. In-fact Khoreshes (stews) taste better the following day, pre-paring food allows the flavors to marinate and infuse. With this said, it is also a good idea to do all your prep-work the day before, if possible. Have all your ingredients measured, marinating, washed, chopped and so on…

How to clean dried barberries (tamiz kardan-e zereshk)

Measure out the amount of berries needed for the recipe. Spread barriers on a large white plate, remove steams and discard any berries that are discolored. Place berries in a bowl of cold water and let soak for 15 minutes. Drain berries in a fine mesh colander. Pat dry and use right away.

Removing Bitterness from eggplants (talkhi gereftan-e badejan)

Eggplants tend to be quite bitter (except for Japanese eggplants). To remove the bitterness from the eggplant: slice the eggplant in half, and place on a tray. Sprinkle sea salt onto the flesh of the eggplant. Leave to stand for 30 minutes, this allows the solanine (a chemical found in the flesh) to be draw out by the salt. Rinse the eggplants with cold water, pat dry, and use as desired.

Saffron Emulsion (Ashapzi Ba Zaferan)

This is a simple secret I was taught from my grandmother, which extends the usage of saffron, with-out losing flavor.

1. Using a mortar or spice grinder, grind 4 pinches of saffron threads with ¼ teaspoon granulated sugar (the sugar aids the saffron to grind properly). Grind until the saffron has reached a fine powder form.
2. Place 2 teaspoons saffron powder in a glass container, add ¼ cup hot water. Stir, cover, and allow liquid to infuse for 15 minutes. Store in a glass dropper bottle in the refrigerator for up to 1 weeks.

homemade butter
kareh

The secret of making the most decadent baked goods, is using homemade butter, the taste is far better than any store bought butter.

Ingredients
2 1/2 cups cold heavy cream
Himalayan salt, to taste
Medium-sized bowl filled with ice water

Method

1. Place heavy cream in the bowl of an electric stand mixer fitted with the whisk attachment. Whip the cream on medium-high for 7 minutes Until the cream separates and the mixture thickens.

2. Using a spatula gather the butter and remove it from the bowl. Note there will still be liquid in the bowl this liquid is actually butter milk. Gather the butter and place it into a double layer of cheesecloth and mold the butter into the shape of a ball. Place ball wrapped in cheesecloth into a bowl of ice water for 5 minutes, remove from water and carefully drain any excess liquid. Sprinkle with salt to taste. Roll butter into a log shape using plastic wrap, and place in a butter dish. Store in the refrigerator and use as needed.

chicken AND vegetable broth

Whenever I prepare a soup or stew I choose to make my own broth. However, if you don't have the time you can opt for an organic, low-sodium prepackaged chicken or vegetable broth.

Ingredients
1 chicken (Do not use for vegetable broth)
2 medium yellow onions, whole
2 celery ribs, cut in half
2 large carrots, washed, cut in half
1 head garlic, cut in half
2 bay leaves
10 peppercorns
5-6 stems from parsley and/or thyme
12 cups water
Salt, to taste

1. Place all ingredients in a large pot, bring to a boil and reduce heat to low, cover and simmer for 2 hours.
2. Remove chicken from pot and set aside for other use.
3. Strain broth through a fine strainer, and discard of the solids.
4. Strain the broth again through a double layer of cheesecloth into a pitcher or another easy-pouring vessel with lid. Refrigerate up to 2 days or freeze, use as needed.
5. If freezing pour the broth into ice cube trays. Once frozen place broth cubes into a ziplock bag, label ziplock bag with date and name item (use within 1 month).

yogurt ~ mast

In a Persian household yogurt is the base for many dishes, this tangy supper food kick-starts the digestive system, thanks to probiotics, and can be used as a face-mask to help clear blemished skin and restore luster to your skin.

Ingredients
8 cups milk
1 cup plain yogurt

Method
1. Place milk into a clean 5-quart saucepan, bring milk to a boil over medium heat.
2. Remove the milk from the heat, let stand until milk is lukewarm.
3. Pour the milk into a heat resistant container with a lid, stir in yogurt, cover with lid, and wrap 2 large clean towels around the bowl.
4. Place the bowl in a warm place and let stand for 12 hours.
5. Keep yogurt in the refrigerator and use as needed for up to a week.
Note: Remember to save 1 cup of yogurt from this batch as a starter for your next batch of yogurt.

Variation:
Thick Yogurt (Mast-e Kisseh)
Pour yogurt into a 2-layer cheesecloth bag, pull the ends together, and hang over a sink or bowl for 25-30 minutes, to allow the excess liquid to drain. When ready the yogurt will have a thick and creamy constancy.

pomegranate molasses ~ rob-e anar

Pomegranate molasses also know as pomegranate syrup, or paste is a thick sweet and sour syrup. That can be used for marinating meat, or added to slow-cooked stews. Although Pomegranate molasses is now readily available in your local grocer, the homemade variety has a better flavor, and doesn't have any added preservatives.

Ingredients
5 cups fresh pomegranate juice
2/3 cups raw honey
1/3 cup lemon juice

Method
1. In a large saucepan place all ingredients, and bring to a boil over high heat, reduce heat to low, let simmer uncovered for 1 ½ -2 hours until the syrup has thickened. Stir occasionally.
2. Remove from heat and set aside to cool. Pour pomegranate molasses into a jar, store in the refrigerator for up to 2 weeks.

hot mint ~ nana dagh

This is a simple sauce/ garnish that is used for soups, stews to add flavor.

Ingredients
4 teaspoons grape seed oil
3 tablespoons fresh mint finely chopped
2 garlic cloves, peeled, crushed

Method
1. In a small sauce pan place grape seed oil, garlic and sauté for 1 minute. Add mint and remove from heat.

caramelized onions ~ *piaz dagh*

Caramelized onions is a garnish used for most aash (soups) and some rice dishes.

Ingredients

4 teaspoons grape seed oil
1 medium onion, peeled, finely sliced
2 teaspoons turmeric
2 garlic cloves, peeled, crushed

1. In a medium saucepan place grape seed oil, onion, turmeric, garlic and sauté for over medium heat, until onions golden.

saffron ghee ~ *roghan-e karfeh*

Ghee, also called clarified butter is added to rice for extra flavor, and is the secret that most Persian restaurants use to make extra decadent rice.

Ingredients

2 sticks (1/2 pound) unsalted butter, cut into small pieces
2 tabelspoons saffron emulsion (see page 37)
1 teaspoon cinnamon

Method

1. In a medium saucepan over low heat, melt the butter slowly. Simmer, and skim off the foam occasionally.

2. Cook until butter in golden, add saffron emulsion, cinnamon and stir with a spoon.

3. Remove the pan from the heat and let stand for 5 minutes. When cool gently pour into a container through a fine mesh strainer or cheesecloth. Store in the refrigerator for up to 2 weeks. Use as needed.

small plates
mezzehs

Mazzeh is Persian for the word taste. Mazzehs are pleasant tastings of small plates that are meant to be an introduction to the meal that proceeds. Traditionally mazzehs are served on a Sofeth (Lace tablecloth), which is spread over a table or a Persian Rug.

yogurt *and* cucumber — *mast'o khiar*

Persians have been partial to this dish since the 11th century, the combination of creamy yogurt, cool cucumber, onions, and mint is just divine. *serves 4*

Ingredients

4 Persian cucumbers, or 1 long English cucumber, peeled, finely chopped
1 small onion, peeled, rinsed, finely chopped
2 cloves garlic, peeled, pressed
2 cup thick yogurt (Mast-e kisseh, lebne or Greek yogurt)
1 tablespoon lemon juice
1 teaspoon dried mint
½ teaspoon Himalayan salt
½ teaspoon freshly ground black pepper

garnish

2 tablespoons dried rose petals

Method

1. In a serving bowl, mix all ingredients together. Cover and refrigerate for 1 hour before serving.

2.. Garnish with rose petals, and serve as an appetizer with lavash.

yogurt and beetroot borani'e labe

This is my favorite Borani, it also makes for a lovely filling for tea-sandwiches. serves 4

Ingredients
1 large or 2 medium beetroot, washed
2 cloves garlic, peeled, pressed
2 cups thick yogurt (Mast-e kisseh, lebne or Greek yogurt)
2 tablespoons sugar
1 tablespoon lemon juice
1 teaspoon dried mint

garnish
2 tablespoons fresh mint, roughly chopped

Method
1. Preheat over to 400 °F.

2. Place beetroot in a rimmed baking sheet lined with parchment paper, sprinkle beetroot with sugar, tightly cover backing sheet with foil. Bake beetroot for 1 hour or until tender.

3. Once cooked, remove beetroots form oven and let cool.

4. Once the beetroot is cool enough to handle, peel and grate beetroot into a serving bowl.

5. Add yogurt, garlic, lemon juice and dried mint to bowl, mix thoroughly. Cover and refrigerate for 20 minutes before serving.

6. Garnish with a mint, serve with pita chips.

45

eggplant and egg spread
mirza ghasemi

This is true Mazandaran (Northern province of Iran) comfort food. A hearty combination of tomatoes, lots of garlic, roasted eggplant, and eggs make up this dip. serves 4-6

Ingredients
2 large eggplants, rinsed, unpeeled
4 cloves garlic, peeled, pressed
4 medium tomatoes peeled and chopped
4 large organic eggs
2 teaspoons turmeric
3 tablespoons extra-virgin olive oil
1 teaspoon Himalayan salt
1 teaspoon freshly ground black pepper

garnish
2 tablespoons fresh basil, roughly chopped

Method
1. Preheat over to 350 °F.

2. Place eggplants in a rimmed baking sheet lined with parchment paper, prick eggplants with a fork and drizzle eggplants with olive oil and a pinch of salt. Bake for 60 minutes.

3. Remove eggplants from oven, and set aside until cool enough to handle (about 30 minutes). Remove the stem, skin and seeds, and chop eggplants finely. Discard the stems, peels, and seeds.

4. In a medium saucepan place 3 tablespoons extra-virgin olive oil, garlic, and turmeric. Sauté until golden over medium heat, place chopped eggplants, tomatoes in saucepan, cover with lid and simmer over medium-low heat for 5 minutes. Stir Occasionally.

5. In a medium bowl place egg yolks, salt, pepper and whisk ingredients together.

6. Pour egg mixture in saucepan with eggplant mixture, stir thoroughly with a wooden spoon. Cook for 8 minutes over low heat.

7. Transfer the mixture to a food processor, and pulse 2-3 times (don't over pulse).

8. Serve warm on a platter alongside yogurt and lavash. Garnish with fresh basil.

feta *and* egg dip ~ panir bereshteh

Panir Bereshteh is a famous recipe from Gilan in the Northern province of Iran. It's so simple to make, and some how so elegant. Serve on a crostini, and this dish makes for perfect hors d'oeuvre for a formal dinner party. *serves 4*

Ingredients

½ Pond feta, rinsed and crumbled
2 tablespoons butter
4 tablespoons fresh dill, finely chopped
2 cloves garlic, peeled, pressed
3 organic eggs
¼ teaspoon turmeric
Pinch of freshly ground pepper

garnish

Sprig of dill

Method

1. In a medium bowl place egg yolks, crumbled feta, chopped dill turmeric, salt, pepper and whisk ingredients together. Set Aside.

2. In a medium saucepan place butter, garlic, and sauté until golden over medium heat. Reduce heat to medium-low, add the egg-feta mixture into the saucepan, and scramble until cooked, about 7 minutes.

3. Transfer the mixture to a food processor, and pulse 2-3 times (don't over pulse).

4. Serve warm on a platter alongside yogurt and lavash. Garnish with fresh dill.

pomegranate marinated olives ~ zeytoon parvardeh

Olives marinated in pomegranate molasses, enough said! This wonderful combination is pure decadence. This recipe comes from northern Caspian Sea, and is traditional made with walnuts. Nevertheless, it is also lovely when made with pistachios. *serves 4*

Ingredients

½ cup kalamata olives, pitted
½ cup green olives, pitted
¼ cup walnuts, or pistachios grated
3 tablespoons extra-virgin olive oil
¼ cup fresh mint, finely chopped
2 tablespoons pomegranate molasses
1 tablespoon raw organic honey

garnish

¼ cup pomegranate arils

Method

1. In a large mixing bowl place olives, grated walnuts, extra-virgin olive oil, chopped mint, pomegranate molasses, honey, and mix together with a spoon until incorporated. Place in an airtight container, and let marinate in the refrigerator for at least 24, preferable 48 hours.

2. To serve: place in a serving bowl, and sprinkle with pomegranate arils. Serve with Feta, and bread.

stuffed grape leaves
dolmehiye barge angur

A Persian dinner party would not be a Persian dinner party without stuffed grape leaves. Persian grape leaves are normally stuffed with ground beef. Nevertheless, I prefer to make them vegetarian as a light mezzeh. Serve Warm or chilled. *serves 4*

Ingredients
1 Jar pickled grape leaves
2 cups long grain rice, soaked for 15 minutes, rinsed, drained
1 cup chopped flat-leaf parsley
1 cup chopped tomato
1 ½ cup fresh lemon juice
½ cup extra virgin olive oil
1/2 cup chopped yellow onion
½ teaspoon cayenne pepper
1 teaspoon Himalayan salt
1/2 teaspoon dried mint
1 pinch ground cinnamon

garnish
Lemon zest

Method
1. Separate leaves and set aside unusable ones.
2. In a medium mixing bowl place rice, parsley, tomato's, ½ cup lemon juice, salt, dried mint, and cinnamon. Mix thoroughly.
3. To roll dolmeh: Place 1 leaf rough side up, remove stem. Place 1 teaspoon of the mixture in the center near the base of the leaf. Fold the stem end over to cover the filling, fold both sides inward lengthwise and then firmly but not to tightly roll grape leaf. Repeat with the remaining leaves and filling.
4. Line an 8-quart saucepan with broken or unusable vine leaves. Place rolled grape leaves on top steam side down, lining from the outside in, so that they are tightly packed. Place a plate on top of the grape leaves, and on top on the plate place a clean heavy rock (this allows the dolma to keep the proper shape when cooking).
5. Place inside pot 1 cup lemon juice, and 1 cup of water, cover with the lid, and bring to a boil over medium high heat. Once at a boil reduce heat to medium low cook for 1 hour.
6. Once dolmas have cooked for an hour add ½ cup extra virgin olive oil, continue cooking for another hour.
7. Remove dolmas from stove, replace plate, leave untouched, and place saucepan in the refrigerator overnight.
8. Place grape leaves on a serving plate, garnish with lemon vest.

herb meatballs — koofteh sabzi

They say the best meatballs are made by a Tabriz (Capital of East Azerbaijan province of Iran) housewife, with this said I learned this recipe from my great grandmother who was born in Tabriz. Serve warm with yogurt. serves 4-6

Ingredients For Meatball

1 pond ground beef or lamb
¼ cup rice, washed
1 cup finely chopped fresh flat-leaf parsley
2 cup finely chopped fresh cilantro
1 cup finely chopped fresh mint
1 large yellow onion, peeled, grated
4 tablespoons tomato paste
2 lemons, juiced
1 teaspoon Himalayan salt
1 teaspoon ground black pepper
1 teaspoon cinnamon
1 teaspoon nutmeg
½ teaspoon turmeric
1 egg

Ingredients For Filling

½ cup sultanas, washed, drained
1 medium yellow onion, finely chopped
Drizzle of extra-virgin olive oil

Method

1. Place rice in a 6-quart saucepan, cover with 3 cups water. Boil rice over medium heat for 15 minutes. Drain, and set aside.
2. In a medium saucepan place chopped medium onion, and a drizzle of extra-virgin olive oil and sauté until onions turn golden. Add sultanas and sauté for 4 more minutes. Remove from heat and set aside.
3. In a large mixing bowl place ground beef, cooked rice, flat-leaf parsley, cilantro, mint, grated onion, and thoroughly mix ingredients together. Add tomato paste, salt, pepper, cinnamon, nutmeg, turmeric, egg, and mix well.
4. Shape the meat mixture into balls about the size of a small tangerine, make a hole in the center of the meatball place 1 teaspoon of sultanas filling. Cover hole with meat mixture, seal, and smooth the outside of the meatballs. Continue until all mixture is used, place each meatball on a tray lined with parchment paper.
5. In a large saucepan drizzle extra-virgin olive oil add ½ of water and lemon juice. Let simmer over medium heat for 10 minutes. Add meatballs to saucepan, cover, let simmer over low heat for 45 minutes, and baste them occasionally with sauce.
6. Place Meatballs on a serving tray serve hot accompanied by Mast-e kisseh (thick yogurt).

chickpea patties with sweet and sour sauce ~ shami

Shami is a donut shaped meat patty seasoned with aromatic spices, served with a sweet and sour sauce. *serves 4-6*

Ingredients For Chickpea Patties

1 pond ground beef, or lamb
1 large yellow onion, peeled, grated
1½ cup chickpea flour, sifted
1 cup cold water
3 organic eggs
½ teaspoon backing powder
½ teaspoon sea salt
½ teaspoon ground black pepper
½ teaspoon cinnamon
½ teaspoon nutmeg
½ teaspoon turmeric
Pinch of saffron threads (grinded & dissolved in 2 tablespoons hot water)
1 cup coconut oil (or more), or any oil for frying

Ingredients For Sauce

3 tablespoons extra-virgin olive oil
1 yellow onion, peeled, finely chopped
4 cloves garlic, peeled, pressed
½ cup white vinegar
½ cup sugar
½ cup water
Pinch of saffron threads (grinded & dissolved in 2 tablespoons hot water)

Method

1. To make the sauce: in a medium-saucepan place the olive oil, chopped onion, garlic, and sauté over medium heat until onions turn golden. Add vinegar, sugar, water, and bring to a boil, reduce heat, and let simmer for 10 minutes. Stir occasionally with a wooden spoon. Add saffron liquid, and set aside.
2. In a small mixing bowl shift chickpea flour, and gradually add the water. Mix until full incorporated. Add salt, black pepper, cinnamon, nutmeg, turmeric, and mix.
3. In a large mixing bowl place ground beef, and gradually and chickpea mixture. Add the eggs, and saffron and continue mixing until full incorporated.
4. Shape the meat mixture into balls about the size of a small tangerine, then flatten in your hand, and poke a hole in the middle using the end of a spoon. Continue until all the mixture is used, place each shami on a tray lined with parchment paper until ready to fry.
5. In a wide medium saucepan place oil, and heat oil over medium-low heat until hot. Fry the patties 5-7 minutes on each side, or until golden brown. Remove the patties with a spotted spoon, and transfer to a plate lined with paper towels. To remove excess oil lightly pat the pastries with a paper towel.
6. Serve warm with the sauce on the side.

lavash potato turnovers
~ samboseh ~

This savory appetizer or snack is simple to make, absurdly easy in fact. Also if you don't have lavash you can make these turnovers with phyllo dough. Serve warm with yogurt. serves 4

Ingredients
2 organic eggs
¼ cup milk
4 sheets of Lavash, cut into 3 x 8-inch strips
1 pound lean ground beef
3 russet potatoes, peeled, rinse, chopped
1 yellow onion, peeled, chopped
2 cloves garlic, peeled, pressed
1 teaspoon turmeric
1 teaspoon cumin
1 teaspoon cayenne pepper
½ teaspoon Himalayan salt
½ black pepper
½ cup fresh flat-leaf parsley, chopped
½ cup fresh mint, chopped

Method
1. In a medium saucepan place chopped onion, garlic, and a drizzle of extra-virgin olive oil and sauté over medium heat until the onions turn golden. Add ground meat, chopped potatoes, turmeric, cumin, cayenne pepper, salt, pepper and sauté for 10 minutes. Add chopped parsley, and mint, and continue to sauté for 5 minutes. Remove from heat, and allow to cool.
2. In a medium mixing bowl place eggs, milk, and whisk until fully incorporated.
3. Adjust oven rack to the middle position, and preheat oven to 350° F. Line one baking sheets with parchment paper, or a non-stick baking mat.
4. On a clean flat surface place the lavash strips. With a pastry brush, brush the strips with the egg mixture. Place one tablespoon of meat filling 1 inch from the end of the pastry. Fold the end over the filling to form a triangle, and continue to fold the strip into triangles (like folding up a flag), when you reach the end of the lavash strip, tuck the remaining edge under, and place onto the prepared baking sheet fold side down spacing each 1-inches apart. Continue until all meat filling is used.
5. When all triangles are folded, brush the tops of the triangles with egg mixture. Bake for 5-7 minutes until golden.

6. Serve warm, with yogurt

aromatic herb salad ∼ sabzi khordan

Sabzi khordan or "eating greens" is a term given to fresh herbs that complements most Persian dishes, and is a lively alternative to the basic green salad. *serves 4*

Ingredients

1 bunch cilantro (ghishniz)
1 bunch flat-leaf parsley (jafari)
I bunch fresh mint (Na'na)
1 bunch fresh spring onion (piazche)
1 bunch sweet basil (reyhan)
1 bunch watercress (sha'ahi)

garnish

1 bunch fresh radish (toropche)

Method

1. Simple remove stems from the cilantro, flat-leaf parsley, mint, sweet basil and watercress. Remove the green parts of the spring onions (you may serve them if desired).

2. Wash herbs thoroughly in cold water, and pat dry with a clean tea towel.

3. To make radish rose garnish: remove the leaves from the radish, clean, and cut off the radish roots and stems. With a paring knife slice four slices down each side of the radish, spacing slices evenly around the radish, make an additional four slices behind the first set of slices. Place radish in a bowl of ice water for 10 minutes, this allows the petals of the radish to open. Continue this process for the rest of the radishes.

4. Place herbs on a platter, garnish with radish roses, and serve.

variation:

Naan-o Paneer-o Sabzi: to the following above add lavash, feta cheese and walnuts, in addition you may warp the ingredients in the lavash for a lovely snack. This is a traditional dish served at a Persian wedding during the Sofreh Aghd.

persian chicken salad
salad'e olivieh

This retro salad was created in Russia by a French chef, and has been adapted to Persian taste. This salad is super comforting both for its speed and its lush creaminess. *serves 4-6*

Ingredients For Salad

2 chicken breast
4 medium potatoes, peeled, rinsed, boiled, chopped into ¾ inch cubes
3 eggs, hard-boiled, mashed
4 dill pickles, finely chopped
4 carrots, peeled, rinsed, steamed, chopped into ½ inch cubes
1 cup green peas, steamed
½ teaspoon turmeric
4 tablespoons extra-virgin olive oil

Ingredients For Dressing

2 cups mayonnaise
¼ cup fresh lemon juice
½ cup extra-virgin olive oil
2 teaspoons mustard
½ teaspoon sea salt
¼ teaspoon freshly ground pepper

garnish

Green Olives

Method

1. In a medium saucepan, place chicken breast, extra-virgin olive oil, and turmeric sauté for 10-15 minutes until cooked. Set aside until cool and the shred the chicken breast.

2. In a large mixing bowl, place mashed eggs, chopped pickles, steamed carrots and peas. Add shredded chicken and combine all ingredients together.

3. In a medium mixing bowl place mayonnaise, lemon juice, extra-virgin olive oil, mustard, sea salt, and freshly ground pepper. Whisk ingredients together.

4. Pour dressing over the salad, and thoroughly mix ingredients together. Refrigerate for 2 hours before serving.

5. Transfer salad into a shallow serving dish. Garnish with olives and serve with lavash.

tomato *and* cucumber salad
salad'e shirazi

This light refreshing and aromatic salad is from Shiraz the capital of Fars Province part of Iran. This salad is a great everyday salad, and pairs well with many rice, and meat dishes. *serves 4-6*

Ingredients For Salad

4 Persian cucumbers (or 2 seedless English cucumbers)
4 medium tomatoes, chopped into ½ inch cubes
½ medium red onion, finely chopped
½ cup fresh mint, roughly chopped

Ingredients For Dressing

2 lemons, juiced
2 tablespoons grape seed oil
½ teaspoon Himalayan salt
½ teaspoon freshly ground black pepper

garnish

¼ cup fresh mint, roughly chopped

Method

1. In a medium mixing bowl place lemon juice, grape seed oil, salt, and freshly ground black pepper. Whisk ingredients together.

2. In a serving bowl place cucumbers, tomatoes, red onions, fresh mint, and mix ingredient together. Pour dressing into the bowl, and toss the salad. Refrigerate for 2 hour before serving.

3. To serve garnish salad with fresh mint atop.

fresh herb frittata ~ kuku-ye sabzi

A beautifully cooked Kuku is one of life's greatest pleasures. As simple as it may sound, it is not always easy to achieve the perfect Kuku. A good kuku must be slightly dense with a velvety texture. Kuku Sabzi is an all-time favorite that is served during Persian New Years. *serves 4-6*

Ingredients

2 cups finely chopped fresh flat-leaf parsley
2 cups finely chopped fresh cilantro
1 cup finely chopped fresh spinach
1 cup finely chopped fresh chives
2 tablespoons yogurt
2 tablespoons zereshk (barberries)
1 teaspoon Himalayan salt
1 teaspoon ground black pepper
1 teaspoon cinnamon
1 teaspoon turmeric
5 organic eggs
¼ cup organic whole milk

garnish

¼ cup crumbled feta

Method

1. Place oven rack to middle Position. Preheat over to 350 °F.

2. In a large mixing bowl place eggs, milk, salt, pepper, cinnamon, and turmeric whisk ingredients together. Add parsley, cilantro, spinach, chives, zereshk, and yogurt. Mix thoroughly.

3. Butter a round 9-inch nonstick cake pan (or a cupcake pan), and pour herb mixture in pan, and smooth the top with a wooden spoon.

4. Bake uncovered for 25 to 35 minutes (if using a cupcake pan 15-20 Minutes), or until a wooden toothpick inserted in the center comes out clean.

5. Cut kuku into wedges, garnish with feta serve warm or chilled accompanied with yogurt.

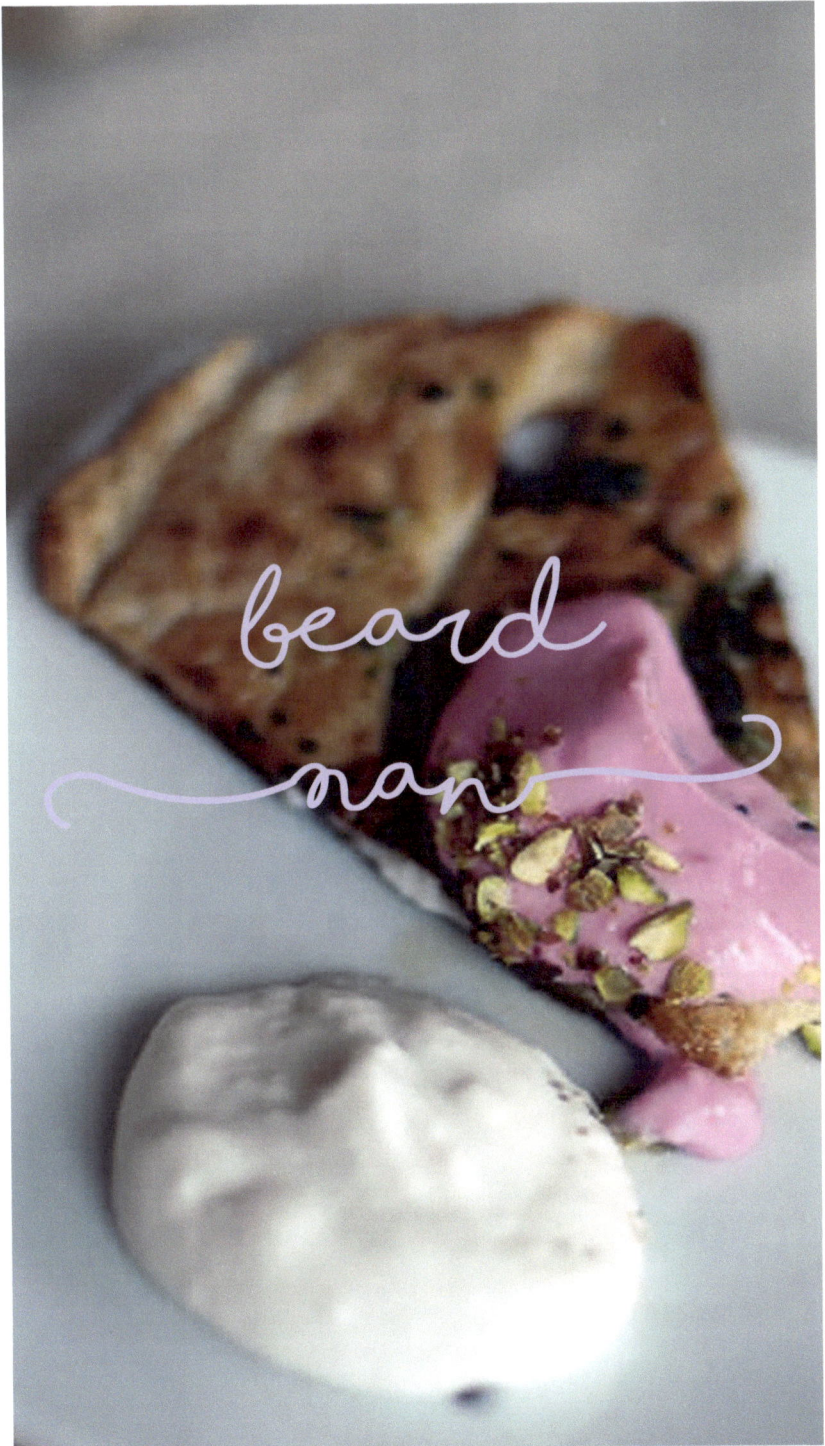

beard nan

Fresh bread is always available in a Persian home, and is served at almost every meal. There are many different types of Persian breads but the stapes are: Lavash, Taftoon, Barbari, Sangak, and Ghandi. I have included all of these recipes, and in addition a recipe for pita bread: pita is not actually a Persian bread. Nevertheless, Persians enjoy it immensely.

lavash flat beard — nan'e lavash

Lavash is a paper Thin, flaky and oval flat bread, and is the oldest known type of bread in the Middle East and Caucasus. Lavash is eaten with all meals. *makes 6*

Yeast Mixture
2 teaspoons active dry yeast
2 tablespoons sugar
½ cup warm water

Dough
6 cups all-purpose flour, sifted
2 teaspoons salt
2 cups warm water

glaze
2 tablespoons extra-virgin olive oil

Method

1. In a medium mixing bowl, place yeast, sugar and warm water. Set aside, and allow to ferment for 10 minutes.

2. In a large mixing bowl place yeast mixture, warm water, salt, and gradually add 6 cups flour while constantly mixing mixture with your hands until a smooth pliable dough is formed (about 15 minutes). Shape dough into a ball, and place dough in a bowl oiled with extra-virgin olive oil. Cover bowl with plastic wrap. Set aside and allow the dough to rise for 35 minutes at room temperature.

3. Adjust oven rack to lowest position, preheat oven to 450° F.

4. Punch down the dough while still in the bowl. Place dough on a clean floured surface, and knead for 7 minutes. Divide dough into six equal parts. Form each part of the dough into a ball. Place each dough ball on a large rimless cookie sheet lined with parchment paper. With a rolling pin, fatten each dough ball into a paper-thin oval as large as the cookie sheet permits. With a fork prick dough allover, and brush bread with extra-virgin olive oil. Brake for 10 minutes or until toasted. Repeat this process for remaining dough.

5. Serve warm or warp in a plastic storage bag.

taftoon flat bread — nan'e taftoon

Taftoon is thin, but thicker than lavash, this nan is soft, round, and sprinkled with nigella seeds. Taftoon Bread is normally made in most Persian homes. *makes 10-11*

Yeast Mixture
2 teaspoons active dry yeast
1 tablespoons sugar
1 cup warm water

Dough
3 cups whole wheat flour, sifted
1 cups all-purpose flour, sifted
¼ cup vegetable oil
1 organic egg
1 teaspoon salt

garnish
2 tablespoons nigella seeds

Method

1. In a medium mixing bowl, place yeast, sugar and warm water. Set aside, and allow to ferment for 10 minutes.

2. In a large mixing bowl place yeast mixture, vegetable oil, egg, salt, and gradually add the flour while constantly mixing mixture with your hands until a smooth pliable dough is formed (about 15 minutes). Shape dough into a ball, and place dough in a bowl oiled with extra-virgin olive oil. Cover bowl with plastic wrap. Set aside and allow dough to rise for 35 minutes at room temperature.

3. Punch down the dough while still in the bowl. Place dough on a cleaned floured surface and knead for 7 minutes. Divide dough into 10-11 equal balls, and roll each ball out to 11-inch circle, and with a fork prick dough allover.

4. In a wide medium saucepan, drizzle extra-virgin olive oil, and heat oil over medium-low heat until hot. Place 1 taftoon into the pan and cook for about 4 minutes on each side. Remove taftoon with tongs, transfer to a plate lined with paper towels. To remove excess oil lightly pat the pastries with a paper towel, and garnish with a sprinkle of nigella seeds. Repeat this process for remaining dough.

5. Serve warm or warp in a plastic storage bag.

barbari bread ~~ nan'e barbari

Barbari bread is a thicker oval-shaped bread, much like focaccia, that is sprinkled with sesame seeds. Barbari Bread is from Tabriz the Capital of East Azerbaijan province of Iran. This bread is also known as Nan-e Tabrizi. This bread is usually eaten for breakfast. Nevertheless, in my home we enjoy it with all meals. *makes 3*

Yeast Mixture
1 package active dry yeast
½ cup warm water
1 tablespoon sugar

Dough
6 cups all-purpose flour, sifted
2 cup warm water
1 teaspoons salt
1 teaspoon baking powder

glaze and garnish
2 egg yolks
¼ cup warm water
2 tablespoons sesame seeds

Method
1. In a medium mixing bowl, place yeast, sugar and warm water. Cover with plastic wrap and set aside for 10 minutes.
2. In a large mixing bowl place yeast mixture, warm water, salt, and gradually add 4 cups flour while constantly mixing mixture with your hands until a smooth elastic dough is formed (about 15 minutes). Shape dough into a ball, and place dough in a bowl oiled with extra-virgin olive oil. Cover bowl with plastic wrap. Set aside and allow dough to rise for 2 hours at room temperature.
3. Adjust oven rack to the middle position, preheat oven to 375° F, and Line three rimless baking sheet with parchment paper, or a non-stick baking mat.
4. Punch down the dough while still in the bowl. Place dough on a floured surface and knead for 10 minutes. Divide the dough into four balls of equal size. Place each dough ball on to onto the prepared baking sheets. With an oiled rolling pin, roll each dough ball out to a 14"x8" inch oval shape. Whit your fingertips make several long dents into the dough.
5. To make glaze: in a small mixing bowl place egg yolks and water and whisk ingredients together. Brush the top of the loaves with glaze, and sprinkle with sesame seeds. Let loaves rest for 10 minutes before placing into preheated oven.

6. Bake for 20 minutes, then turn over and bake for additional 10 minutes, and repeat this process for remaining dough.

7. Serve warm or warp in a plastic storage bag

61

sangak bread ~ nan'e sangak

Sangak bread is a stone-baked thin oval-shaped bread, that is sprinkled with nigella seeds, and cumin. To correctly make this bread you will need a baking stone, and a baker's peel. *makes 4*

Yeast Mixture
1 package active dry yeast
2 ½ cup warm water
1 tablespoon sugar

Dough
3 cups whole-wheat flour, sifted
1 ¼ cup all-purpose flour, sifted
1 teaspoons salt

glaze and garnish
Drizzle of grape seed oil
2 tablespoons nigella seeds
2 tablespoons ground cumin

Method

1. In a Large mixing bowl, place yeast, sugar and warm water. Cover with plastic wrap and set aside for 10 minutes.

2. Shifted the whole-wheat flour, all-purpose flour, and salt together. Next gradually add sifted flour into the large bowl, while constantly mixing mixture with your hands until sticky dough is formed (about 15 minutes). Shape dough into a ball, and place dough in a bowl oiled with grape seed oil. Cover bowl with plastic wrap. Set aside and allow dough to rise for 6 hours at room temperature.

3. Adjust oven rack to the lowest position, and place the baking stone. Preheat oven to 450° F.

4. Punch down the dough while still in the bowl. Place dough on a oiled surface and knead for 10 minutes. Divide the dough into four balls of equal size. With an oiled rolling pin, roll each dough ball out to a 1/2-inch thick oval. Using a floured baker's peel place the dough on one end of the peel. Using your fingertips make indents on top of the dough. Brush the top of the loaf with grape seed oil, and sprinkle with nigella seed, and cumin.

5. Place the loaf on top of the hot baking stone, bake for 2 minutes, using the bakers peel press dough on the loaf, and bake for 2 minutes, and then flip with the bakers peel and continue baking for 2 minutes. Remove loaf from oven, and repeat this process for remaining loafs.

6. Serve warm or warp in a plastic storage bag.

pita bread ~ nan'e pita

Pita is a flat round bread that puffs up when baking to create a cute little pocket. When baking if your first pitas don't puff, place 10-15 ice cubes on a backing sheet, and place baking sheet on the lowest rack under the pita you are baking (this will yield steam, allowing the pitas to puff), and continue backing. *makes 10*

Yeast Mixture
1 package active dry yeast
½ cup warm water
1 tablespoon sugar

Dough
3 ½ cups all-purpose flour, sifted
1 cup warm water
1 teaspoons salt

glaze & garnish
2 egg yolks
¼ cup warm water

Method

1. In a medium mixing bowl, place yeast, sugar and warm water. Cover with plastic wrap and set aside for 10 minutes.

2. In a large mixing bowl place yeast mixture, warm water, salt, and gradually add 3 ½ cups flour while constantly mixing mixture with your hands until a elastic lightly sticky dough is formed (about 7 minutes). Shape dough into a ball, and place dough in a bowl oiled with extra-virgin olive oil. Cover bowl with plastic wrap. Set aside and allow dough to rise for 2 hours at room temperature.

3. Adjust oven rack to the lowest position, preheat oven to 450° F, and Line two rimless baking sheet with parchment paper, or a non-stick baking mat.

4. Punch down the dough while still in the bowl. Place dough on a floured surface and knead for 5 minutes. Divide the dough into ten balls of equal size. With a floured rolling pin, roll each ball into a round shape approximately ¼ inch thick. Place pitas loaves onto the prepared baking sheets.

5. To make glaze: in a small mixing bowl place egg yolks and water and whisk ingredients together. Brush the top of the loaves with glaze, and Let pitas rest for 5 minutes before placing into preheated oven.

6. Bake for 10 minutes on each side, and repeat this process for remaining dough. Serve warm.

sweet rose flat bread
nan'e ghandi

Ghandi bread is thin round, and sweet with a hint of ginger. This bread is served during breakfast with tea. *makes 14*

Yeast Mixture
1 package active dry yeast
2 cups sugar
½ cup warm water

Dough
7 cups all-purpose flour, sifted
1 cup whole milk
1 cup heavy cream
¼ cup rosewater
1 teaspoons salt
1 teaspoon baking powder
1 teaspoon ground cinnamon
1 teaspoon ground ginger
½ ground cardamom

garnish
¼ cup confectioner's sugar

Method

1. In a large mixing bowl, place yeast, sugar and warm water. Cover with plastic wrap and set aside for 10 minutes.

2. Add milk, heavy cream, rosewater, salt, baking powder, ground cinnamon, ground ginger, and ground cardamom into the yeast mixture, and mix ingredients together using a whisk. Gradually add 7 cups flour while constantly mixing mixture with your hands until a smooth pliable dough is formed (about 15 minutes). Place dough on a floured surface and knead for 15 minutes. Shape dough into a ball, and place dough in a bowl oiled with extra-virgin olive oil. Cover bowl with plastic wrap. Set aside and allow dough to rise overnight in a warm, dark place.

3. Punch down the dough while still in the bowl. Place dough on a cleaned floured surface and knead for 7 minutes. Divide the dough into 14-15 equal balls, and roll each ball out to 11-inch circle, and with a fork prick dough allover.

4. In a wide medium saucepan, drizzle extra-virgin olive oil, and heat oil over medium-low heat until hot. Place 1 ghandi into the pan and cook for about 4 minutes on each side. Remove ghandi with tongs, transfer to a plate lined with paper towels. To remove excess oil lightly pat the pastries with a paper towel, and garnish with a sprinkle with confectioner's sugar. Repeat this process for remaining dough.

5. Serve warm or warp in a plastic storage bag.

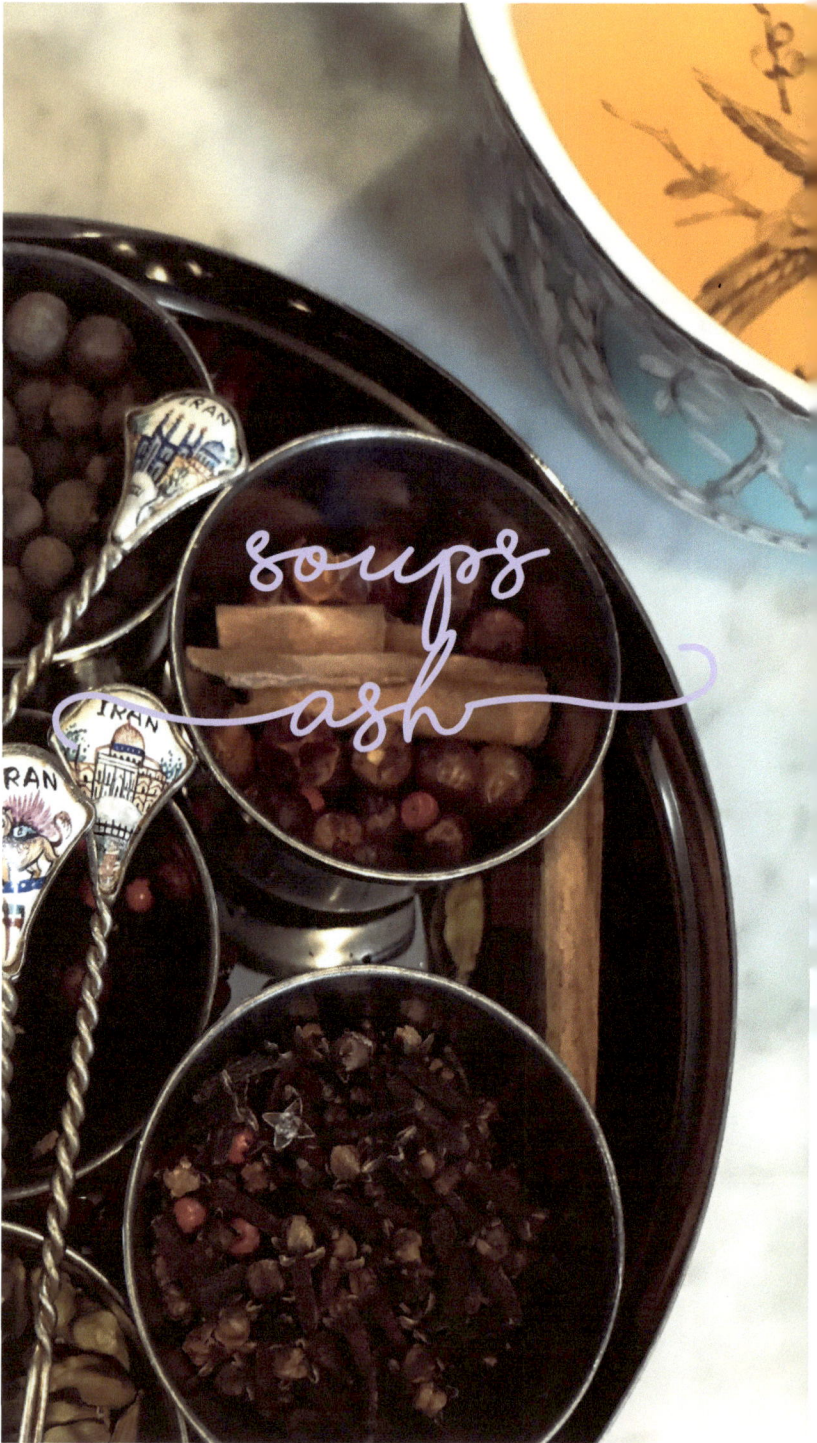

soups

ash

Theres something about soups that is just so old school, so cozy, so heartwarming, and most of all so delicious. Ash in Farsi means soup, and soup is the heart of Persian cooking. As indicated in the Farsi word for cook ashpaz, which literally meaning maker of Soup. There are three cooking styles for preparing Persian soups The first is Ash a harder soup filled with nutrition and is often eaten as a main course. The second is abgusht a thin soup with a meat-base, and the third simple being called soup, a French bisque style creamy soup that has been adapted to Persian taste.

As a general rule, all Persian soups can be prepared a day in advance, refrigerated, and reheated the next day

pomegranate soup — ashie anar

This is my mothers' recipe. She would make this soup on the coldest of winter days, those days when your body aches, and you fancy a comfy shawl, and lots of warm soup. This hearty sweet-and-sour aromatic soup can be mad with or with-out the mini meatballs either way it's wonderful. *serves 6-8*

Soup Ingredients
2 ½ cups Kidney beans, soaked overnight, rinsed, drained
½ cup rice, soaked overnight, rinsed, drained
1 cup chopped fresh flat-leaf parsley, roughly chopped
1 cup chopped fresh cilantro, roughly chopped
½ cup fresh mint, roughly chopped
2 tablespoons rose water
2 cups pomegranate juice
4 tablespoons extra-virgin oil
1 tablespoons angelica powder (gol-par)
1 tablespoon pomegranate molasses
1 teaspoon cinnamon
¼ teaspoons sea salt

Meatballs Ingredients
1 pound ground beef
1 egg
½ cup fresh mint
1 large yellow onion, peeled, rinsed, grated
¾ cup chickpea flour
1 teaspoon cinnamon
½ teaspoon turmeric
½ teaspoon sea salt
½ teaspoon freshly ground black pepper

garnish
Na'na dagh (page 40)
½ cup pomegranate seeds
1 dollop of thick yogurt

Method
1. In a 6-quart saucepan place a drizzle of extra-virgin olive oil, add onions, cinnamon, and Sauté until onions turn golden. Add water, Kidney beans, and bring to a boil over high heat. Reduce heat to medium, cover and simmer for 30 minutes. Add rice and cook for 20 minutes longer.
2. In a large mixing bowl, place ground beef, egg, mint, onion, cinnamon, chickpea flour, turmeric, salt, pepper, and thoroughly mix ingredients together. Using a melon baller, roll meat mixture into 1-inch meatballs.
3. Gently place meatballs to saucepan, add flat leaf parsley, cilantro, and mint. Cover with lid, simmer for 20 minutes, and stir occasionally.
4. Stir in pomegranate juice, rose water, and angelica powder, simmer and reduce heat to low. Let simmer for 15 minutes.
5. Transfer soup into a tureen, garnish with Na'na dagh, thick yogurt, and pomegranate seeds.

noodle soup ashie reshteh

This gorgeous, velvety and restorative noodle soup is traditional made during Persian New Years. In Persian culture noodles are believed to bring good fortune. serves 6-8

Ingredients

½ pond linguine noodles
1 cup kidney beans, soaked in water overnight, rinsed, drained
1 cup chickpeas, soaked in water overnight, rinsed, drained
½ cup red lentils, rinsed, drained
3 cups fresh spinach, roughly chopped
2 cups fresh flat-leaf parsley, roughly chopped
1 cup fresh cilantro, roughly chopped
4 cloves garlic, peeled, minced
2 yellow onions, peeled, rinsed, chopped
¾ cup kashk (sun dried yogurt)
6 cups chicken broth

2 cups water
4 tablespoons extra-virgin olive oil
2 teaspoons dried mint
1 teaspoon turmeric
1 teaspoon sea salt
½ teaspoon fresh ground black pepper
Pinch of saffron threads (grinded & dissolved in 2 tablespoons hot water)

garnish

Na'na Dagh (page 40)
Piaz Dagh (page 41)
¼ cup kashk (sun dried yogurt)

Method

1. 1. In a 6-quart saucepan place a drizzle of extra-virgin olive oil, add onions, garlic, tomatoes, salt, pepper, and sauté over medium heat until onions turn golden. Add kidney beans, chickpeas, and turmeric. Pour in chicken broth, and water into saucepan. Bring to a boil over medium heat, and simmer for 45 minutes. Add lentils and cook for another 20 minutes. Stir occasionally with a spoon.

2. Place reshteh into the saucepan cook for 10 minutes. Add spinach, flat-leaf parsley, cilantro, dried mint, stir, and cook for 15 minutes.

3. Adjust the thickness of the ash if to thick add water. Stir in saffron liquid and kashk (sun dried yogurt). Simmer for 5 minutes uncovered.

4. To serve ladle ash into a soup tureen and garnish with na'na dagh, piaz dagh, and kashk.

wedding soup ~ soup'e aroosi

This soup is served traditionally at Persian wedding parties (Aroosi) in Tabriz, the capital of East Azerbaijan Province of Iran. It is said that if a young girl makes a wish to find a husband while eating this soup, she will be married within the next year. *serves 6-8*

Ingredients

1 pond stew meat beef, or lamb
2 yellow onions, peeled, rinsed, chopped
4 carrots, peeled, rinsed, grated
1 lemon, juiced
½ cup yogurt
2 eggs
Pinch of saffron threads (grinded & dissolved in 2 tablespoons hot water)
1 teaspoon sea salt
½ teaspoon fresh ground black pepper
8 cups water

garnish

Dollop of yogurt

Method

1. In a 6-quart saucepan place a drizzle of extra-virgin olive oil, add onions, garlic, carrots, salt, pepper, and sauté over medium heat until onions turn golden. Add beef, turmeric and seal meat on all sides. Pour water into saucepan. Bring to a boil over medium heat, and simmer for 2 hours. Stir Occasionally.

2. In a medium-mixing bowl, place yogurt, saffron emulsion, eggs, lemon juice, and whisk ingredients together.

3. Pour yogurt mixture into soup 7 minutes before serving.

4. Serve the ash in a shallow bowl, and garnish with a dollop of yogurt.

tender lamb with pulses soup
abgusht

When I am in the mood for a robust traditional meal, there's nothing more satisfying than Abgust. This dish can typically be found at road side caravanserai, and is customarily made in large clay pots. The traditional way to serve this dish is to strain the broth and serve it as soup, with the solids on the side. Moreover, some people like to mash the solids together to create paste for dipping bread in. This dish is always served with sangak, or barbari bread.

serves 6-8

Ingredients

4 lamb shanks
2 yellow onions, peeled, rinsed, chopped
1 cup kidney beans, soaked in water overnight, rinsed, drained
1 cup chickpeas, soaked in water overnight, rinsed, drained
2 dried limes, washed, dried, pierced with a fork
4 medium potatoes, peeled, cut in half
4 tablespoons tomato paste
4 tablespoons extra-virgin olive oil
2 teaspoons turmeric

1 teaspoon sea salt
½ teaspoon fresh ground black pepper
1 lemon, juiced
Pinch of saffron threads (grinded & dissolved in 2 tablespoons hot water)
8 cups water

Method

1. In a 6-quart saucepan place a drizzle of extra-virgin olive oil, add onions, salt, pepper, and sauté over medium heat until onions turn golden. Add lamb shanks, turmeric and seal meat on all sides.

2. Add the 8 cups water, kidney beans, chickpeas, bring to a boil, and reduce heat to low. Cook for two hours, until the lamb shanks and beans are fully cooked. Stir occasionally.

3. Add the tomato paste, cut potatoes, stir, and let simmer for 1 hour. Stir occasionally.

4. Add lemon juice, let simmer for another 5 minutes, and just before serving add the saffron liquid.

5. Serve the Abgusht with Barbari or Sangak Bread, and sabzi khordan.

71

tomato soup ~ soup'e gojeh farang

Serve this spicy tomato soup warm or chilled, along-side toasted Barbari Bread sprinkled with feta. *serves 4*

Ingredients
5 cups ripe tomatoes, chopped
1 yellow onion, chopped finely
4 cups chicken broth
1 cup heavy cream
3 teaspoons honey
2 teaspoons ground cloves
1 teaspoon turmeric
1 teaspoon sea salt
½ teaspoon cayenne pepper
2 tablespoons extra-virgin olive oil

garnish
Dollop of yogurt

Method
1. In a 6-quart saucepan place a drizzle of extra-virgin olive oil, add tomatoes, onions, and sauté until onions turn golden. Add honey, ground cloves, turmeric, salt, and cayenne pepper. Pour in chicken broth and heavy cream into saucepan. Bring to a boil over medium heat, and simmer for 15 minutes. Stir Occasionally.

2. Puree soup with an immersion blender until smooth. Adjust seasoning to taste.

3. To serve ladle soup into serving bowls and garnish with a dollop of yogurt.

saffron cream of rice soup
soup'e berenji

This is a lovely warming, creamy rich soup that happens to be one of my most prided recipes. The saffron adds a luxurious depth to this basic soup. . serves 4

Ingredients

1 cup basmati rice, soaked 2 hours, rinsed, drained
4 cups organic low sodium chicken broth
2 cups whole milk
½ cup heavy cream
5 tablespoons flour
4 tablespoons of unsalted butter
1 teaspoon grated nutmeg
½ teaspoon sea salt
½ teaspoon fresh ground black

garnish
Sprig of Dill

Method

1. In a 6-quart saucepan place rice, and chicken broth. Cover saucepan, bring to a boil over medium heat, and simmer for 25 minutes. Stir occasionally.

2. In a medium saucepan, melt the butter over low heat, once butter is melted add flour and stir with a wooden spoon. Stir until there are no lumps. Increase the heat to medium-low. Slowly pour milk in to saucepan while constantly whisking. Add heavy cream and continue whisking ingredients until creamy. Remove from heat and stir in salt, pepper and nutmeg, and set aside.

3. Pour milk into a 6-quart saucepan cook for 45 minutes, and stir occasionally. With an immersion blender partially puree soup. Just before serving add the saffron liquid, and mix.

4. Ladle ash into shallow bowls, garnish with a sprig of dill.

persian matzo ball soup
gondi

This soup is a traditional Persian Jewish dish: much like an eastern European matzo ball soup. Persian Matzo balls are made from roasted chickpea flour, and is a favorite among most Persians.
serves 4-6

Ingredients For Broth
5 cups chicken broth
2 cups water
3 yellow onions, peeled, rinsed, left whole
4 carrots, peeled, rinsed, chopped in half
¼ cup fresh lime juice
1 teaspoon turmeric
1 teaspoon sea salt
½ teaspoon fresh ground black pepper

Ingredients For Matzo ball
1 pond ground chicken (dark-meat
2 yellow onions, peeled, rinsed, grated
1 large organic egg
1 cup chickpea flour
1 teaspoon turmeric
1 teaspoon cumin
1 teaspoon ground cardamom
2 tablespoons extra-virgin olive oil

Method

1. In a 6-quart saucepan place a drizzle of extra-virgin olive oil, add onions, salt, pepper, and sauté over medium heat until onions turn golden. Add chicken broth, water, onions, carrots, lime juice, turmeric, salt, and pepper. Cover saucepan, bring to a boil over medium heat, and simmer for 25 minutes. Stir occasionally.

2. In a large mixing bowl place ground chicken, onions, egg yolk chickpea flour, turmeric, cumin, cardamom, extra-virgin olive oil and thoroughly mix ingredients together. Shape the meat mixture into balls about the size of a small tangerine.

3. Gently place meatballs into saucepan. Cover with lid, simmer for 35 more minutes, and stir occasionally.

4. Ladle gondi in a shallow bowl serve warm.

creamy turkey porridge with cinnamon & haleem

This hidden gem of a recipe is basically peasant food, that warms you up from head to toe, and is perfect for a cold winter morning. This aromatic porridge is ridiculously simple to prepare, and is pretty much foolproof. When serving top with a knob of butter, a pinch of brown sugar and ground cinnamon. serves 4-6

Ingredients

Drizzle of extra-virgin olive oil
1 pond skinless turkey breast
1 yellow onion, thinly sliced
½ teaspoon turmeric
1 ½ cup pre-shelled bulgur
4 cups water
4 tablespoons light brown sugar
2 teaspoons ground cinnamon
pepper
Pinch of saffron threads (grinded & dissolved in 2 tablespoons hot water)

garnish

Pinch of light brown sugar
Pinch of ground cinnamon
knob of butter

Method

1. In a 6-quart medium sauté pan over medium heat, drizzle extra-virgin olive oil, place the sliced onions, brown sugar, ground cinnamon, and sauté onions until golden brown. Add the turkey breast, turmeric, and sauté for 15-25 minutes until cooked. Remove turkey, and set aside until cool, and then shred the turkey breast.

2. Add the bulgur, and 4 cups of water, and bring to a boil over medium heat for 20 minutes. Stir occasionally.

3. Reduce heat to low, add the shredded cooked chicken, and continue to cook for 15 minutes, and stir occasionally. Using an immersion blender puree the porridge.

4. Ladle the porridge into individual serving bowls, garnish each bowl with brown sugar, ground cinnamon, and a knob of butter.

stews
khoreshes

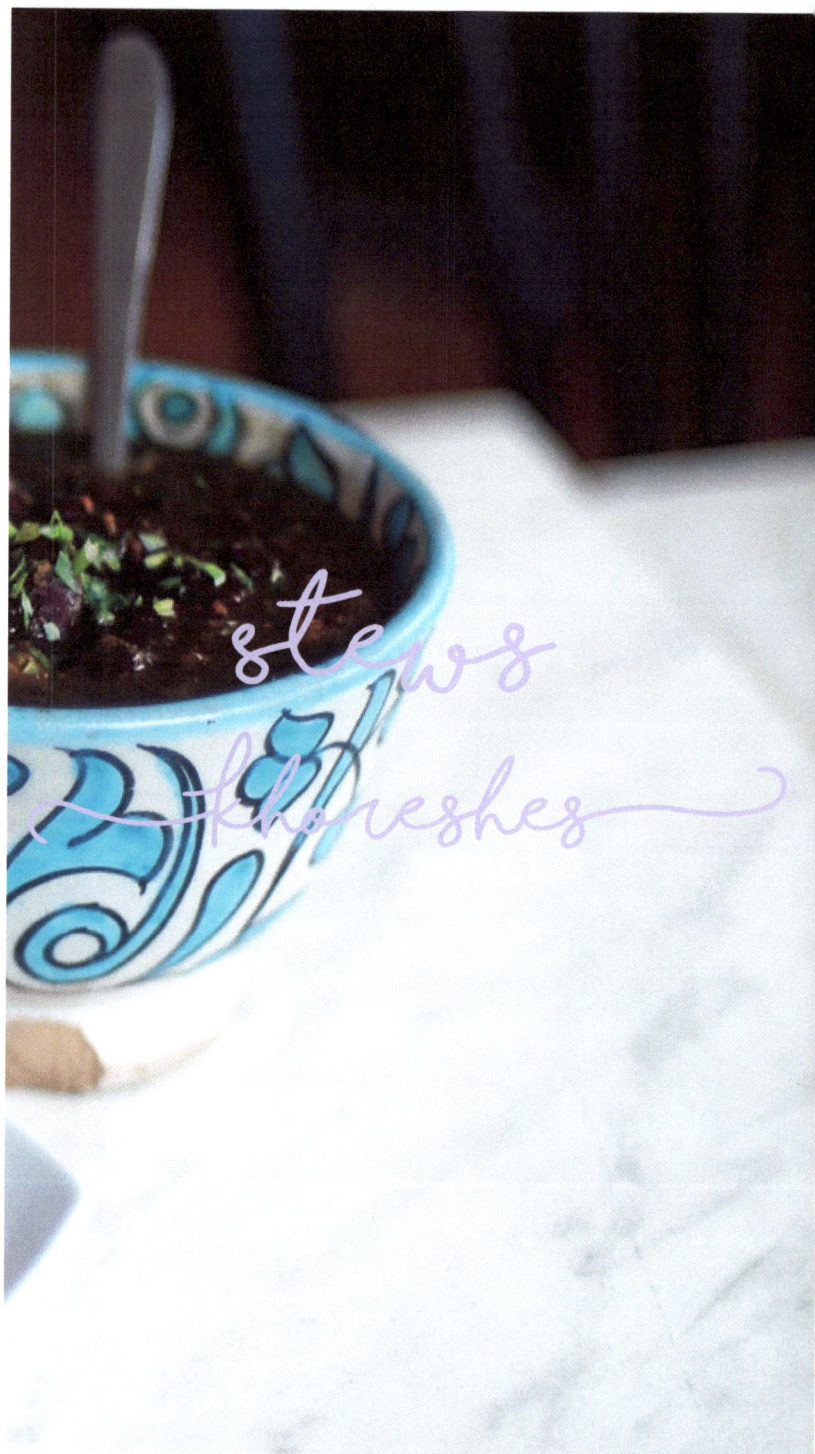

Khoreshes are mild stews no guilty oozing fatty juice maple wholesome produce. Nevertheless these mild meals are always present at parties even at the most elegant wedding galas. The basic khoreshes will consist of a combination of ingredients such as meat or poultry with warming spices aromatic herbs, pulses and or greens. The more rare khoreshes will feature fresh and or dried fruits and nuts.

Khoreshes differ from region, and are always cooked with the freshest ingredients of the season, making for a lovely delicious meal with great depth and nutritional balance.

The Khoreshes from Northern Iran by the Caspian Sea tend to have more complex flavor combinations, featuring rich voluptuous sauces.
Whereas Khoreshes from the South by the Persian Gulf use purer spices and tend to have a thinner liquidy sauce.

When preparing though you must cook the stew over a low flame very gently. Only stirring every so often. Khoreshes are best prepared a day in advance so that the flavours can develop properly. Reheat the following day just before serving.

Khoreshes are always served along side or atop of chelo (Persian white rice)

spinach and golden plum stew
khoreshie esfenajo alu zard

This recipe is r dedicated to Shafie khanoom. I have such found memories of her making this splendid stew. *serves 4-6*

Ingredients

2 ponds stew meat beef, or lamb cut into 2-inch cubes
2 ponds fresh spinach, washed, lightly chopped
3 cups golden dried plums (Alu Zard), pitted
2 yellow onions, peeled, rinsed, thinly sliced
2 ½ cups water
½ cup fresh lemon juice
4 tablespoons extra-virgin olive oil
1 ½ teaspoon turmeric
1 teaspoon sea salt
½ teaspoon fresh ground black pepper
Pinch of saffron threads (grinded & dissolved in 2 tablespoons hot water)

Method

1. In a 6-quart saucepan place onions, extra-virgin olive oil, turmeric, and sauté over medium heat until onions turn golden. Add the meat, salt, pepper and sauté for 5 minutes while browning meat on all sides. Pour in water and lemon juice, cover saucepan, and simmer for 1 hour over low heat. Stir occasionally with a wooden spoon.

2. Add Spinach, and dried plums, cover, and cook for another 35 minutes, and stir occasionally.

3. Stir in saffron liquid and simmer for 5 minutes uncovered.

4. Serve warm accompanied by chelo (Steamed rice).

quince stew ~ khoreshe beh

This is a glorious for lack of a better word "yummy" stew. I simply love the process of this stew, it's quite a treat to see the yellow quinces magically turn a robust red.. *serves 6*

Ingredients

1½ ponds stew meat beef, or lamb cut into
2-inch cubes
4 Large quinces rinsed (not peeled), cored, and
sliced into wedges
2 yellow onions, peeled, rinsed, thinly sliced
2 potatoes, peeled, rinsed, chopped
6 oz tomato paste
1 cup pitted prunes
3 cups water
½ cup fresh lemon juice
4 tablespoons extra-virgin olive oil
1 ½ teaspoon turmeric
1 teaspoon cinnamon
1 teaspoon sea salt
½ teaspoon fresh ground black pepper

Method

1. In a 6-quart saucepan place onions, extra-virgin olive oil, 1. In a 6-quart saucepan onions, extra-virgin olive oil, turmeric, cinnamon and sauté over medium heat until onions turn golden. Add the stew meat, quinces, salt, pepper and sauté for 5 minutes while browning meat on all sides. Pour in water and lemon juice. Cover saucepan, and simmer for 1 hour over low heat. Stir occasionally with a spoon.

2. Add prunes, potatoes, and tomato paste. Cover, cook for another 35 minutes. Stir occasionally.

3. Serve warm accompanied by chelo (Steamed rice).

variation:

Peach Stew (Khoresh'e Hulu): Follow the above recipe. However, replace the quinces for 4 peaches, and in step 1 eliminate the potatoes, and tomato paste, and reduce the cooking time to 35 minutes. Continue to follow instructions as directed.

aromatic herb love stew
khoreshie gormeh sabzi

My recipe for Gormeh Sabzi is second to none. This dish is an ancient aphrodisiac due to the fenugreek, and according to my mamani (gradmother) if you want a man to fall in love with you make him Gormeh Sabzi. serves 6

Ingredients

2 pounds filet mignon, or lamb cut into 1-inch cubes
2 yellow onions, peeled, rinsed, thinly sliced
4 garlic cloves, peeled, finely minced
2 cup fresh spinach, roughly chopped
2 cups fresh flat-leaf parsley, roughly chopped
1 cup fresh mint, roughly chopped
1 cup fresh cilantro, roughly chopped
½ cup fresh fenugreek, roughly chopped, or 3 tablespoons fenugreek
½ kidney beans, soaked in water overnight, drained
5 cups water
½ cup fresh lime juice
4 whole dried limes (limu-omani), pierced
4 tablespoons extra-virgin olive oil
1 ½ teaspoon turmeric
½ teaspoon sea salt
½ teaspoon fresh ground black pepper

Method

1. In a 6-quart saucepan place onions, extra-virgin olive oil, turmeric, and sauté over medium heat until onions turn golden. Add the filet mignon, salt, pepper and sauté for 5 minutes while browning meat on all sides. Pour in water and lemon juice. Add drained kidney beans, and dried limes. Cover saucepan, and simmer for 1 hour over low heat. Stir occasionally with a spoon.

2. In a medium sauté pan place a drizzle of extra-virgin olive oil, add spinach, flat-leaf parsley, mint, cilantro, and fenugreek. Sauté over medium heat, string constantly for 5 minutes.

3. Add the Sauté herb mixture into the 6-quart saucepan and let simmer for 15 more minutes.

4. Serve warm accompanied by chelo (Steamed rice).

pomegranate *and* walnut stew
khoresh'e fesenjan

This special yet simple stew is from the Caspian region of Iran. This stew is a delightful mix of rich pomegranate juice, walnuts, and tender bite-size pieces of chicken. *serves 6*

Ingredients
4 skinless boneless chicken breast, cut into
2-inch cubes
1 yellow onions, peeled, rinsed, chopped
2 cups shelled walnuts
4 cups fresh pomegranate juice
½ cup fresh lime juice
4 tablespoons extra-virgin olive oil
2 teaspoons cinnamon
1 teaspoon turmeric
1 teaspoon sea salt
½ teaspoon fresh ground black pepper
Pinch of saffron threads (grinded & dissolved in 2
tablespoons hot water)

garnish
½ cup pomegranate seeds

Method
1. Finely grind walnuts in a food processor.

2. In a 6-quart saucepan place onions, extra-virgin olive oil, cinnamon, turmeric, and sauté over medium heat until onions turn golden. Add chicken breast, salt, pepper and sauté for 5 minutes. Pour in pomegranate juice, and lime juice. Cover saucepan, and simmer for 1 hour over low heat. Stir occasionally with a spoon.

3. The khoresh should be sweet and sour, and have a creamy consistency. If khoresh is too thick add ½ pomegranate juice.

4. Add saffron liquid, and let simmer uncovered for 5 minutes.

5. Serve warm in a casserole dish, garnish with pomegranate seeds accompanied by chelo (Steamed rice).

yellow split pea and potato stew
khoreshe geymeh

Do you know the feeling when you eat something so good you can't wait to have it again? Well that's how most people feel once they have had khoresh-e Geymeh. This very wholesome stew is layered with tomatoes, delicate yellow split peas, tender pieces of meat, and laced with saffron, and Omani. While topped with ultra-thin herbed fries. *serves 6*

Ingredients

1 ½ ponds stew meat beef, or lamb cut into 2-inch cubes
2 yellow onions, peeled, rinsed, thinly sliced
½ cup yellow split peas, soaked in water for 2 hours
6½ cups water
¼ cup fresh lime juice
5 whole dried limes (limu-omani), pierced
4 tablespoons extra-virgin olive oil
4 tablespoon tomato paste
1 teaspoon cinnamon
1 ½ teaspoon turmeric

1 teaspoon sea salt
½ teaspoon fresh ground black pepper
Pinch of saffron threads (grinded & dissolved in 2 tablespoons hot water)

garnish

2 large potatoes, peeled, rinsed
Drizzle of extra-virgin olive oil
Pinch of Sea salt
½ cup fresh flat-leaf parsley, roughl chopped

Method

1. In a 6-quart saucepan place onions, extra-virgin olive oil, turmeric, cinnamon, and sauté over medium heat until onions turn golden. Add the stew meat, salt, pepper and sauté for 5 minutes. Pour in 3½ cups water and lime juice. Add the dried limes. Cover saucepan, and simmer for 1 hour over low heat. Stir occasionally with a spoon.
2. In a 2-quart saucepan place drained yellow split peas, 3 cups water, and a pinch of salt. Cook for 30 minutes, and drain.
3. Place cooked yellow split peas and tomato paste into the 6-quart saucepan, and simmer over low heat for 30 minutes. Add saffron liquid, and let simmer uncovered for 5 minutes before serving.
4. Adjust oven rack to medium position, preheat oven to 425° F.
5. Using a mandoline, slice the potatoes into ultra-thin strips (shoestrings). Then gently pat dry fries with a paper towel. Place fires on a large rimless cookie sheet lined with parchment paper. Drizzle fires with extra-virgin olive oil and a pinch of sea salt. Bake for 18 minutes or until crisp and golden brown. Remove from oven and set aside.
6. Serve warm in a shallow serving dish, garnish with fries and flat-leaf parsley, accompanied by chelo (Steamed rice).

assyrian curry stew
khoreshie cari

This delicious Assyrian stew gets its flavor and fragrance from the tart yogurt and exotic hints of curry and turmeric. *serves 6*

Ingredients

2 ponds skinless boneless chicken breast, cut into 1½-inch pieces
2 medium yellow onions, peeled, rinsed, thinly sliced
4 garlic cloves, peeled, finely minced
2 cups water
3 cups thick yogurt (mast)
½ cup fresh lemon juice
5 tablespoons medium hot curry powder
1 tablespoon flour
1 teaspoon ground coriander
1 teaspoon grated fresh ginger
4 tablespoons extra-virgin olive oil

1 ½ teaspoon turmeric
½ teaspoon sea salt
½ teaspoon fresh ground black pepper
Pinch of saffron threads (grinded & dissolved in 2 tablespoons hot water)

Method

1. In a 6-quart saucepan place onions, garlic, extra-virgin olive oil, turmeric, curry powder, coriander, and sauté over medium heat until onions turn golden. Add chicken breast, salt, pepper and sauté for 5 minutes. Pour in 2 cups water and lemon juice. Cover saucepan, and simmer for 1½ hours over low heat. Stir occasionally with a spoon.

2. In a medium-mixing bowl, place yogurt, saffron liquid and whisk ingredients together.

3. Add yogurt mixture to 6-quart saucepan and simmer for 5 minutes over low heat.

4. Serve Khoresh warm in a shallow serving dish, accompanied by chelo (Steamed rice).

tangerine chicken stew
khoreshe narengi

This dish is traditionally made with the Persian citrus fruit naranja: a very sour orange. In English this fruit is know as the Seville orange, or bitter orange. For this recipe I use tangerines with lemon juice to compensate for the naranja since they are hard to find. However if you are able to find naranjas by all means us it in replacement of the tangerines and lemon juice. . serves 6

Ingredients

2 ponds skinless boneless chicken breast, cut into 1½-inch pieces
1 medium yellow onion, peeled, rinsed, thinly sliced
1 cup fresh tangerine juice
1½ fresh tangerine peels, Julienned into thin strips
2 tangerines, cut into segments
½ cup fresh lemon juice
2 tablespoons granulated sugar
Drizzle of extra-virgin olive oil

1 teaspoon turmeric
½ teaspoon sea salt
½ teaspoon freshly ground black pepper
Pinch of saffron threads (grinded & dissolved in 2 tablespoons hot water)

Method

1. In a medium sauté pan over medium heat, place the julienned tangerine peels, with 2 cups water and bring to a boil for 4 minutes. Drain and repeat process 2 more times (this removes the bitterness from the tangerine peels).

2. In a 6-quart saucepan place a drizzle of extra-virgin olive oil, drained tangerine peels, sugar, and sauté over medium heat for 2 minutes. Add the onions turmeric, salt, pepper, and sauté until onions turn golden. Add chicken breast, tangerine juice, lemon juice. Cover the saucepan, and simmer for 1½ hours over low heat. Stir occasionally with a spoon.

3. Add saffron liquid, and tangerine segments, and simmer for 10 minutes over low heat.

4. Serve Khoresh warm in a shallow serving dish, accompanied by chelo (Steamed rice).

eggplant stew — khoreshe bedemjane

This is classic Persian comfort food at its best. The mixture of grilled eggplant, tomatoes, fork tender meat, and tart unripe grapes creates a lovely, rich, full flavored stew. *serves 6*

Ingredients

3 medium eggplants
2 pounds stew meat beef, or lamb
2 yellow onions, thinly sliced
4 garlic cloves, peeled, finely minced
4 medium tomatoes, halved
6 tomatoes, copped
3 whole dried limes (limu-omani), pierced
1 cup fresh unripe grapes (ghureh)
1 heaped tablespoon tomato paste

2 cups water
¼ cup fresh lemon juice
1½ teaspoon turmeric
½ teaspoon sea salt
½ teaspoon fresh ground black pepper
Pinch of saffron threads (grinded & dissolved in 2 tablespoons hot water)

Method

1. Pell each eggplant, and cut lengthwise into four slices. Place eggplant slice on a backing tray lined with parchment paper. Sprinkle each eggplant piece with salt, and leave for 15 minutes. With a paper towel pat dry the eggplant pieces to remove excess salt. Set aside.

2. In a 6-quart saucepan place onions, garlic, extra-virgin olive oil, turmeric, and sauté over medium heat until onions turn golden. Add the stew meat, salt, pepper, and brown meat on all sides. Add the dried limes, the chopped tomatoes, tomato paste, and water. Cover saucepan, and simmer for 1½ hour over low heat. Stir occasionally with a spoon.

3. Meanwhile, in a medium wide sauté pan place a drizzle of extra-virgin olive oil, add eggplant pieces and sauté over medium heat until eggplants are golden brown. Add halved tomatoes, unripe grapes, and sauté for 30 seconds. Remove sauté pan from the heat.

4. Place the sautéed eggplant mixture into the 6-quart saucepan. Add the saffron liquid, and lemon juice and let simmer gently for 15 more minutes.

5. Serve warm accompanied by chelo (Steamed rice).

green bean stew ⌐ khoreshie lubia

This stew is a stable in most Persian homes, finding its way to the dinner table at least once a week. serves 6

Ingredients

2 pounds stew meat (beef, or lamb),
cut into 2-inch cubes
1 pound fresh green beans, trimmed
2 yellow onions, thinly sliced
2 garlic cloves, peeled, finely minced
2 heaped tablespoon tomato paste
2 cups water
1 ½ teaspoon turmeric
½ teaspoon cinnamon
½ teaspoon sea salt
½ teaspoon fresh ground black pepper
Pinch of saffron threads (grinded & dissolved in 2 tablespoons hot water)

Method

1. In a 6-quart saucepan place onions, garlic, extra-virgin olive oil, turmeric, cinnamon and sauté over medium heat until onions turn golden. Add the stew meat, salt, pepper and brown meat on all sides. Add the tomato paste, and water. Cover saucepan, and simmer for 45- minutes over low heat. Stir occasionally with a spoon.

2. Meanwhile, in a medium wide sauté pan place a drizzle of extra-virgin olive oil, add green beans and sauté over medium heat for 2 minutes. Remove sauté pan from the heat.

3. Place the sautéed green beans into the 6-quart saucepan. Add the saffron liquid, and let simmer for 35 minutes, or until meat is tender.

4. Serve warm accompanied by chelo (Steamed rice).

sour cherry stew khoreshie albaloo

Sour cherries and lemon juice gives this stew a fresh-tanging taste.

Ingredients

2 ponds skinless boneless chicken
breast, cut into 1½-inch pieces
1 medium yellow onions, peeled,
rinsed, thinly sliced
2 garlic cloves, peeled, finely minced
2 cups sour cherries, pitted
3 cups water
½ cup fresh lemon juice
1 teaspoon cinnamon
1 teaspoon brown sugar
1 teaspoon turmeric
½ teaspoon sea salt
½ teaspoon fresh ground black
pepper
Pinch of saffron threads (grinded &
dissolved in 2 tablespoons hot water)

garnish

Drizzle of organic raw honey

Method

1. In a 6-quart saucepan place onions, garlic, extra-virgin olive oil, turmeric, cinnamon, brown sugar, and sauté over medium heat until onions turn golden. Add chicken breast, salt, pepper and sauté for 5 minutes. Pour in 1 cups water and lemon juice. Cover saucepan, and simmer for 1½ hours over low heat. Stir occasionally with a spoon.

2. Add the cherries, saffron liquid and simmer for 10-15 minutes over low heat.

4. Serve Khoresh warm in a shallow serving dish, drizzle with honey, a serve accompanied by chelo (Steamed rice).

rhubarb and mint stew
khoresh'e riyas

Persians are quite fond of rhubarb, and rhubarb is actually native to Iran. This stew has a sweet-and-sour flavor combination that is truly unique. *serves 6*

Ingredients

1 ponds stew meat beef, or lamb cut into 2-inch cubes
1 pond fresh rhubarb stalks, peeled, slices crosswise into 3-inch long pieces
2 yellow onions, peeled, rinsed, thinly sliced
2 tablespoons tomato paste
3 cups organic low sodium vegetable stock
¼ cup fresh lemon juice
4 tablespoons extra-virgin olive oil
2 cups flat-leaf parsley, roughly chopped
½ cup fresh mint, roughly chopped
1½ teaspoon turmeric
½ teaspoon sea salt
½ teaspoon fresh ground black pepper
½ tablespoon raw organic honey
Pinch of saffron threads (grinded & dissolved in 2 tablespoons hot water)

Method

1. In a 6-quart saucepan onions, extra-virgin olive oil, turmeric, and sauté over medium heat until onions turn golden. Add the stew meat, salt, pepper and sauté for 5 minutes. Pour in vegetable stock, cover saucepan, and simmer for 1 hour over low heat. Stir occasionally with a wooden spoon.

2. In a medium sauté pan place a drizzle of extra-virgin olive oil, add flat-leaf parsley, and mint. Sauté over medium heat, string constantly for 5 minutes.

3. Add the Sautéed herb mixture into the 6-quart saucepan. Add the cut rhubarb, lemon juice, honey, saffron liquid, and let simmer for 25 more minutes. Stir occasionally with a spoon.

4. Serve warm accompanied by chelo (Steamed rice)

variation:

Celery Stew (Khoresh'e Karafs): Follow the above recipe. However, replace the rhubarb for celery. Continue to follow instructions as directed.

spicy tamarind fish stew
ghalieh mahi

This stew is from khoosestan, a region in the Southern part of Iran where they like their food prepared on the spicy side. *serves 6*

Ingredients

2 ponds salmon, cut into 2-inch pieces
2 cups fresh cilantro, roughly chopped
1 cup fresh fenugreek, roughly chopped, or 2 tablespoons dried fenugreek
1 yellow onion, finely sliced
2 garlic cloves, peeled, finely minced
2 tablespoons tamarind paste
2 ½ cups hot water
¼ cup fresh lemon juice
4 tablespoons extra-virgin olive oil
1 teaspoon cayenne pepper
1½ teaspoon turmeric
½ teaspoon sea salt
½ teaspoon fresh ground black pepper

Method

1. In a large sauté pan onions, extra-virgin olive oil, turmeric, and sauté over medium heat until onions turn golden. Add garlic, cayenne pepper, and stir. Add the chopped cilantro, chopped fenugreek, and sauté while string constantly for 5 minutes.

2. Place the tamarind paste into the hot water, and pour the mixture into the sauté pan. Cover the sauté pan, and let simmer for 15-20 minutes. Reduce heat to medium low.

3. Gently place the fish into the sauté pan, and cook for 25-30 minutes. Make sure not to stir the stew. Adjust the seasoning to taste.

4. In a medium sauté pan place a drizzle of extra-virgin olive oil, add flat-leaf parsley, and mint. Sauté over medium heat, string constantly for 5 minutes.

5. Serve warm accompanied by chelo (Steamed rice).

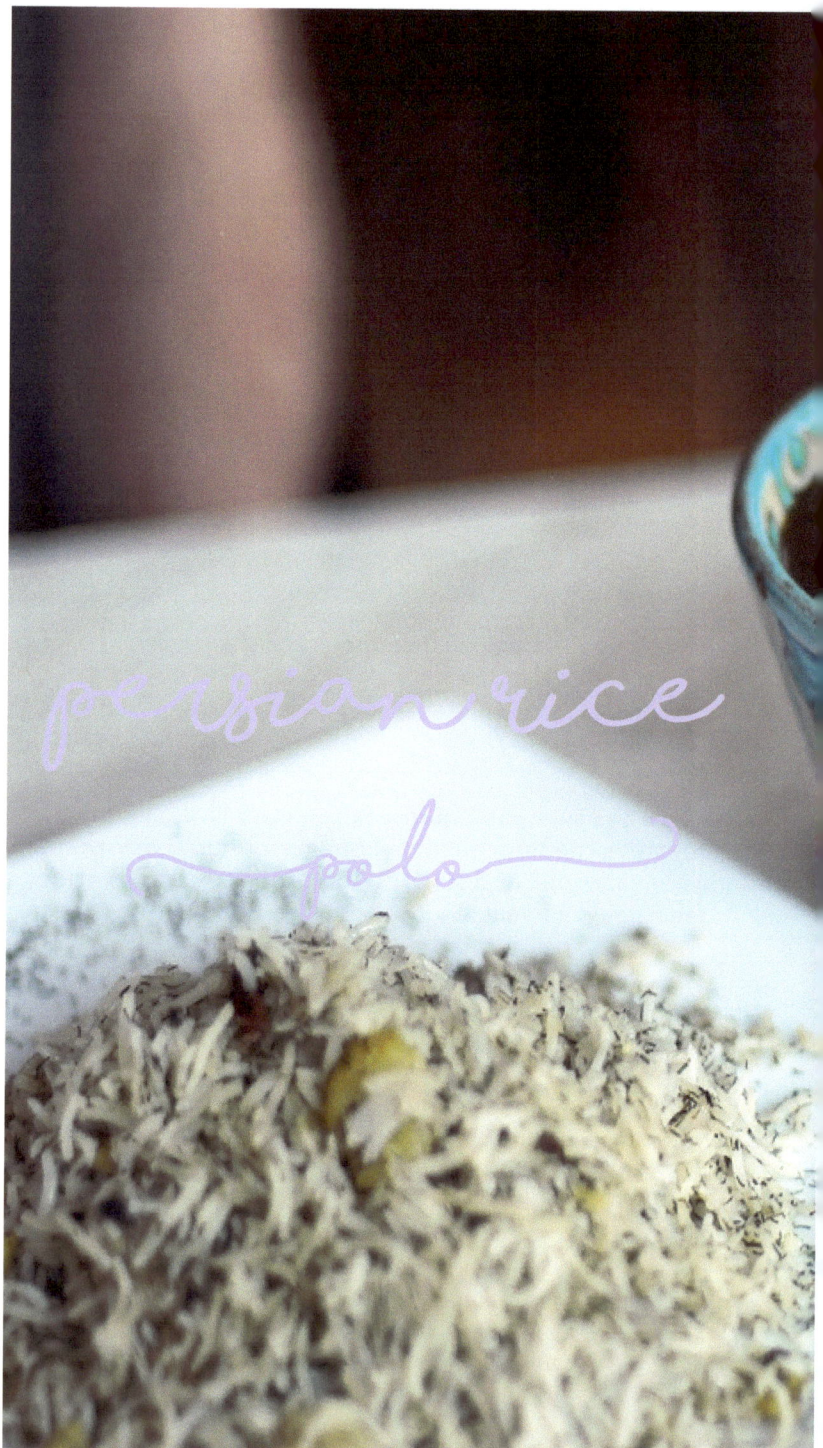

persian rice

polo

Preparing rice is like painting a picture. Rice itself is a blank canvas that can transform into a staple or an elaborate dish depending on the ingredients added. Persian rice dishes are lavishly layered with spices, aromatic herbs, floral waters, fresh vegetables, fresh and dried fruits, and or nuts. There are three main styles for cooking rice: Chelo, Polo, and Kateh. With this said all of the above styles for preparing rice yields only a crunchy golden decadent rice crust.

Chelo is white rice par boiled, and then steamed to fluffy perfection yielding an aromatic individually grained non sticky rice. Chelo is traditionally served with koresht and kabobs.

Polo is chelo rice adorned with an array of fresh herbs, vegetables, pulses, fruits, nuts, and meat, or chicken. Polos are served at weddings, formal occasions, or as added elegance to any meal. Polos can be served as a main dish or as a side dish.

Kateh is Persian sticky rice. This style of rice cookery comes from the northern part of Iran by the Caspian Sea where rice is grown. This style of rice is informal and is only served at family dinners and never served to guest.

*Also please note: When handling cooked rice use a slotted spoon.

saffron steamed rice
chelo

This golden-crusted rice is the heart and soul of Persian cooking. This simple dish is served daily with basically every meal. The delicate taste of the infused saffron mixed with the rice empowers your senses – it's the simplicity of these ingredients that make this dish so special. serves 6

Ingredients For Rice
Drizzle of extra-virgin olive oil
4 cups long-grain basmati rice, soaked in water
for 2 hours, rinsed, drained
1 tablespoon salt
8 cups water

Ingredients For Crust (Tadig)
¼ cup saffron ghee (page 41), divided

Method
1. In a 6-quart saucepan place 8 cups water. Bring to a boil over high heat. Once at a boil pour drained rice, salt, and a drizzle of extra-virgin olive oil into the saucepan.
2. Boil for exactly 10 minutes, drain rice in a large, fine-mesh colander and risen with cold water. Set Aside.
3. In a 4-quart nonstick sauté pan, place ¼ cup of saffron ghee, and spread over the enter bottom of the pan. Gently place rice into the sauté pan, distributing rice evenly, and gradually shaping rice into the shape of a pyramid. Drizzle the rest of the saffron ghee over the rice, distributing it evenly.
4. Warp the lid of the 4-quart nonstick sauté pan in a clean tea towel, and place lid tightly on the pan. Steam over medium heat for 20 to 25 minutes.
5. Remove from heat, place sauté pan in a large stainless steel mixing bowl half way filled with ice water (this helps to free the tadig), and let cool for 5 minutes.

plating chelo
There are two ways to unmold and serve chelo:
The first is to hold a flat serving platter tightly over the uncovered sauté pan, and invert the cooked rice onto the serving platter (like inverting a cake out of a pan).

The second way is to gently remove the rice with a spatula, placing rice on a serving platter, while molding the rice into the shape of a pyramid. Detach the layer of crust (tadig) from the bottom of the sauté pan with a spatula, and arrange crust (tadig) around the rice platter.

variations:

Rice Crust (Tadig) Variations For Step 3: The variations listed below for tadig can be used for all polo recipes.

Yogurt Crust: In a medium mixing bowl place 1 cup parboiled rice, ½ yogurt, ¼ cup saffron ghee and mix ingredients together. Spread the mixture on to the bottom of the sauté pan, and continue to follow the recipe.

Milk Crust: In a medium mixing bowl place 1 cup parboiled rice, ½ cup milk, ¼ cup Saffron ghee, and mix ingredients together. Spread the mixture on to the bottom of the sauté pan, and continue to follow the recipe.

Egg Crust: In a medium mixing bowl place 1 cup parboiled rice, 2 egg yolks, ¼ cup Saffron ghee, and mix ingredients together. Spread the mixture on to the bottom of the sauté pan, and continue to follow the recipe.

Lavash Crust: Place ¼ cup saffron ghee in a sauté pan, and spread saffron ghee over the enter bottom of the pan. Place a layer of lavash bread on the bottom of the sauté pan (make sure lavash covers the entire bottom of the pan), and continue to follow the recipe.

Potato Crust: Peel and slice potatoes into 1/8 inch thick slices. Place ¼ cup saffron ghee in sauté pan, and spread saffron ghee over the enter bottom of the pan. Place sliced potatoes on the bottom of the sauté pan, and continue to follow the recipe. Please note that you can substitute the potatoes for any root vegetable.

jeweled rice
javaher polo

This decadent wonderful dish, is rich and voluptuous, and always a special meal. Javaher Polo also called Marasa Polo it is typically served at weddings, engagement parties and other joyous celebrations. This dish is called jeweled rice because of the combination of jeweled colored ingredients glistening like gems atop a bed of fluffy rice. Javaher Polo is the Shah (King) of all Persian rice dishes, and is a feast for your eyes as well as your belly. *serves 6*

Ingredients For Rice

4 cups long-grain basmati rice, soaked in water for 2 hours, rinsed, drained
8 cups water
¼ cup saffron ghee (page 41)
½ cup slivered almonds, soaked in water for 1 hour, drained
½ cup slivered pistachios, soaked in water for 1 hour, drained
1½ cup shredded orange peels, soaked in boiling water for 5 minutes, drained and rinsed.
2 cups shredded carrots
½ cup sultanas
1 cup barberries, cleaned

Ingredients For Rice

1 granulated sugar
4 tablespoons Persian Rice Spice Mix (page 34)
2 tablespoons orange blossom water
Pinch of saffron threads (grinded & dissolved in 2 tablespoons hot water)
1 tablespoons sea salt
Drizzle of extra-virgin olive oil

Ingredients For Crust
(Tadig)

½ cup saffron ghee (page 41)
2 tablespoons orange blossom water
Pinch of saffron threads (grinded & dissolved in 2 tablespoons hot water)

Method

1. In a medium nonstick sauté pan drizzle extra-virgin olive oil, place drained almonds, pistachios, and sauté for 1 minute over medium heat. Remove mixture from sauté pan, and set aside.

2. In the same nonstick sauté pan drizzle extra-virgin olive oil, place sultanas, barberries, 4 tablespoons of sugar, and 2 tablespoons orange blossom water. Sauté for 1 minute, while stirring constantly (barberries burn quickly), remove from heat, and set aside.

3. Heat ¼ cup saffron ghee in a large nonstick sauté pan over medium heat. Add drained orange peels, shredded carrots, and. Sauté for 2 minutes. Add 1 cup sugar, ½ cup water, 2 teaspoons saffron liquid, and cook over medium heat for 10-15 minutes (until sugar dissolves and all liquid is absorbed.

jeweled rice
javaher polo

4. In a 6-quart saucepan place 8 cups water, and salt. Bring to a boil over high heat. Once at a boil pour drained rice, and 2 tablespoons extra-virgin olive oil into the saucepan. Boil for exactly 10 minutes, drain rice in a large, fine-mesh colander and risen with cold water. Set Aside.

5. In a medium mixing bowl place 1 cup parboiled rice, ¼ cup saffron ghee, 2 tablespoons orange blossom water, and mix ingredients together. Spread the mixture onto the bottom of a medium nonstick sauté pan.

6. Gently place 2 spatulas of parboiled rice into the pan, next sprinkle 2 tablespoons Persian Rice Spice mix over rice, and then place 1 spatula of orange peel and shredded carrot mixture. Repeat layering the parboiled rice, spice mixture, and orange peel mixture, distributing ingredients evenly, gradually shaping race into the shape of a pyramid. Drizzle the remaining saffron ghee, and saffron liquid over the rice.

7. Warp the lid of the nonstick sauté pan in a clean tea towel, and place lid tightly on the pan. Steam over medium heat for 30 to 35 minutes.

8. Serve on a shallow platter; gently mounding rice into the shape of a pyramid, garnish atop with candied barberries, sultanas, and nut mixture. Alternately, you can mix all ingredients together.

9. Detach the layer of crust (tadig) from the bottom of the sauté pan with a spatula, arrange crust (tadig) on a small platter, and serve on the side.

variation:

Sweet Saffron Rice (Shirin Polo): Follow the above recipe, except eliminate all ingredients from Step 2.

sour cherry rice — albaloo polo

I love Albaloo polo, it's a staple in my home. This fluffy aromatic sweet and sour rice is simply delicious. I like to sever this rice with kababe joojeh (chicken kabob), or koobideh (ground beef kabob). serves 6

Ingredients For Rice

3 cups long-grain basmati rice, soaked in water for 2 hours, rinsed, drained
8 cups water
2 ponds fresh/frozen sour cherries, pitted, stems removed, cleaned
½ cup granulated sugar
¼ cup lime juice
2 tablespoons ground cinnamon

2 tablespoons rose water
Pinch of saffron threads (grinded & dissolved in 2 tablespoons hot water
1 tablespoons sea salt
2 teaspoons of extra-virgin olive oil

Ingredients For Crust
(Tadig)

½ cup saffron ghee (page 41)
2 tablespoons rose water
Pinch of saffron threads (grinded & dissolved in 2 tablespoons hot water

Method

1. In a medium nonstick sauté pan, place sour cherries, sugar, rose water and lime juice, gradually bring to a boil over high heat and cook for 10 minutes. Remove from heat and strain sour cherries over a bowl, while saving the syrup. Set both items aside.

2. In a 6-quart saucepan place 8 cups water, and salt. Bring to a boil over high heat. Once at a boil pour drained rice, and 2 tablespoons extra-virgin olive oil into the saucepan. Boil for exactly 10 minutes, drain rice in a large, fine-mesh colander and risen with cold water. Set Aside.

3. In a medium mixing bowl place 1 cup parboiled rice, ¼ cup saffron ghee, 2 tablespoons rose water, and mix ingredients together. Spread the mixture onto the bottom of a medium nonstick sauté pan.

4. Gently place 2 spatulas of parboiled rice into the pan, next sprinkle 1 tablespoons ground cinnamon over rice, and then place 1 spatula of drained sour cherries. Repeat, alternating layers of the parboiled rice, ground cinnamon, sour cherries, while gradually shaping rice into the shape of a pyramid. Drizzle the remaining saffron ghee, and saffron liquid over the rice.

5. Warp the lid of the nonstick sauté pan in a clean tea towel, and place lid tightly on the pan. Steam over medium heat for 30 to 35 minutes.

6. Remove lid from sauté pan and pour ¼ cup cherry syrup over the rice, cover and cook for another 10 minutes.

7. Serve rice on a shallow platter, gently mounding rice into the shape of a pyramid. Detach the layer of crust (tadig) from the bottom of the sauté pan with a spatula, and arrange crust (tadig) around the rice platter.

barberry saffron rice
zereshk polo

Whenever I make Zereshk polo I like to serve it with a chicken dish. The tangy berries pairs nicely with tender chicken. *serves 6*

Ingredients For Rice

3 cups long-grain basmati rice, soaked in water for 2 hours, rinsed, drained
6 cups water
¼ cup saffron ghee (page 41)
2 cup barberries, cleaned
4 tablespoons granulated sugar
2 tablespoons Persian Rice Spice Mix (page 34)
2 tablespoons rose water
1 tablespoons sea salt

Ingredients For Crust

(Tadig)
¼ cup saffron ghee (page 41)
Pinch of saffron threads (grinded & dissolved in 2 tablespoons hot water

Method

1. In a nonstick sauté pan, place ¼ cup saffron ghee, barberries, 4 tablespoons of sugar, and 2 tablespoons rose water. Sauté for 1 minute, while stirring constantly (barberries burn quickly), remove from heat, and set aside.
2. In a 6-quart saucepan place 8 cups water, and salt. Bring to a boil over high heat. Once at a boil add drained rice, and 2 tablespoons extra-virgin olive oil into the saucepan. Boil for exactly 10 minutes, drain rice in a large, fine-mesh colander and risen with cold water. Set Aside.
3. In a medium mixing bowl place 1 cup parboiled rice, ¼ cup saffron ghee, 2 tablespoons rose water and mix ingredients together. Spread the mixture onto the bottom of a medium nonstick sauté pan.
4. Gently place 2 spatulas of parboiled rice into the pan, then sprinkle 2 tablespoons Persian Rice Spice mix over the rice. Repeat these steps, while gradually arranging the rice into the shape of a pyramid. Drizzle the remaining saffron ghee, and saffron liquid over the rice.
5. Warp the lid of the nonstick sauté pan in a clean tea towel, and place lid tightly on the pan. Steam over medium heat for 30 to 35 minutes.
6. Place rice on a serving platter in alternating layers with barberry mixture. Mound the rice into the shape of a pyramid. Detach the layer of crust (tadig) .

fava bean and dill rice
baghala polo

There are meals that leave a mark, forever engraved in your mind, and for me Baghala Polo is that dish. This dish reminds me of spring the fluffy white rice layered with tender fava beans, and lots of freshly chopped dill are just a wonderful flavor combination.

serves 6

Ingredients For Rice

4 cups long-grain basmati rice, soaked in water for 2 hours, rinsed, drained
8 cups water
4 cups shelled Fava beans, fresh or frozen
6 cups fresh dill weed, finely chopped
1 teaspoon turmeric
Pinch of saffron threads (grinded & dissolved in 2 tablespoons hot water)
1 tablespoon sea salt

Ingredients For Crust

(Tadig)

¼ cup saffron ghee (see page 41)
2 egg yolks
Pinch of saffron threads (grinded & dissolved in 2 tablespoons hot water

Method

1. In a 6-quart saucepan place 8 cups water, turmeric, and salt. Bring to a boil over high heat. Once at a boil pour rice, fava beans, and 2 tablespoons extra-virgin olive oil into the saucepan. Boil for exactly 10 minutes, drain rice in a large, fine-mesh colander and risen with cold water Set Aside.

2. In a medium mixing bowl place 1 cup parboiled rice, 2 egg yolks, ¼ cup saffron ghee, and mix ingredients together. Spread the mixture onto the bottom of a nonstick sauté pan.

3. Gently place 2 spatulas of rice-fava bean mixture into the pan, then place 1 cup dill, distributing dill evenly. Repeat these steps, while gradually arranging the rice in the shape of a pyramid. Drizzle the remaining saffron ghee, and saffron liquid over the rice.

4. Warp the lid of the nonstick sauté pan in a clean tea towel, and place lid tightly on the pan. Steam over medium heat for 30 to 35 minutes.

5. Place rice on a serving platter. Detach the layer of crust (tadig) from the bottom of the sauté pan, and arrange crust (tadig) around the rice platter.

red rice with fillet mignon estamboli polo

Simple ingredients, healthy, robust with flavor, and easy to prepare - this is the perfect rice dish to serve as a main meal. *serves 6*

Ingredients For Rice

1 ½ pounds filet mignon, cut into 1-inch cubes
4 cups long-grain basmati rice, soaked in water for 2 hours, rinsed, drained
8 cups water
¼ cup fresh lime juice
6 medium tomatoes peeled, finely chopped
1 large yellow onion, peeled, rinsed, finely chopped
4 cloves of garlic, peeled, minced
3 tablespoons tomato paste

3 tablespoons extra-virgin olive oil
2 tablespoons Persian Rice spice mix (page 34)
2 tablespoons sea salt
1 teaspoon turmeric
½ teaspoon cayenne

Ingredients For Crust

(Tadig)
¼ cup saffron ghee (see page 41)
Pinch of saffron threads (grinded & dissolved in 2 tablespoons hot water)

Method

1. In a medium sauté pan place onions, garlic, extra-virgin olive oil, Persian rice spice mix, turmeric, cayenne, and sauté over medium heat until onions turn golden. Add the filet mignon, and sauté for 5 minutes. Pour in lime juice, Add tomatoes, and tomato paste. Cover saucepan, and simmer for 30 minuets over low heat. Stir occasionally with a wooden spoon. Set aside.

2. In a 6-quart saucepan place 8 cups water, and salt. Bring to a boil over high heat. Once at a boil pour in drained rice, and 2 tablespoons extra-virgin olive oil into the saucepan. Boil for exactly 10 minutes, drain rice in a large, fine-mesh colander and risen with cold water. Set Aside.

3. In a medium mixing bowl place 1 cup parboiled rice, ¼ cup Saffron ghee and mix ingredients together. Spread the mixture onto the bottom of a large nonstick sauté pan.

4. Gently place 2 spatulas of parboiled rice mixture into the pan, in alternating layers with meat-and-tomato mixture. Repeat these steps, while gradually arranging the rice in the shape of a pyramid. Drizzle the rest of the saffron ghee, and saffron liquid over the rice.

5. Warp the lid of the nonstick sauté pan in a clean tea towel, and place lid tightly on the pan. Steam over low heat for 50 minutes.

6. Place rice on a serving platter, and arrange crust (tadig) around the rice platter.

variation:

Green Bean Rice (Lubia Polo): Follow the above recipe, except add 1 pond fresh French green beans cut into ¼ inch length pieces, and 1 teaspoon limu-omani (dried Persian lime powder) to step 1. Continue to follow instructions as directed.

aromatic herb rice — sabzi polo

This dish is traditional made for Norooz (Persian New Years) and is served with white fish. *serves 6*

Ingredients For Rice

4 cups long-grain basmati rice, soaked in water for 2 hours, rinsed, drained
8 cups water
2 tablespoons extra-virgin olive oil
2 cups fresh flat-leaf parsley, finely chopped
3 cups fresh cilantro, finely chopped
2 cups fresh dill weed, finely chopped
1 cup fresh chives, finely chopped
6 cloves of garlic, peeled, minced
2 tablespoons dried fenugreek

1 tablespoons sea salt
1 teaspoon turmeric
½ teaspoon ground cumin
½ teaspoon ground cinnamon

Ingredients For Crust

(Tadig)

¼ cup saffron ghee (see page 41)
2 egg yolks
Pinch of saffron threads (grinded & dissolved in 2 tablespoons hot water)

Method

1. In a large mixing bowl place flat-leaf parsley, cilantro, dill weed, chives, fenugreek, garlic and mix ingredients together. Add turmeric, cumin, cinnamon, thoroughly mix ingredients. Set aside.

2. In a 6-quart saucepan place 10 cups water, and salt. Bring to a boil over high heat. Once at a boil pour drained rice, and 2 tablespoons extra-virgin olive oil into the saucepan. Boil for exactly 10 minutes, drain rice in a large, fine-mesh colander and risen with cold water. Set Aside.

3. In a medium mixing bowl place 1 cup parboiled rice, 2 egg yolks, ¼ cup Saffron ghee, and mix ingredients together. Spread the mixture onto the bottom of a medium nonstick sauté pan.

4. Gently place 2 spatulas of parboiled rice mixture into the pan, in alternating layers with herb mixture. Repeat these steps, while gradually arranging the rice in the shape of a pyramid. Drizzle the rest of the saffron ghee, and saffron emulsion over the rice.

5. Warp the lid of nonstick sauté pan in a clean tea towel, and place lid tightly on the pan. Steam over medium heat for 30 to 35 minutes.

6. Place rice on a serving platter, and arrange crust (tadig) around the rice platter.

sweet milk rice ～ shir polo

Growing up whenever I had an upset stomach my grandmother would make me this sticky sweet aromatic rice to heal my tummy ache. I like to serve this rice for breakfast, and a late-night delight. *serves 6*

Ingredients For Rice

2 cups long-grain basmati rice, soaked in water for 2 hours, rinsed, drained
4 cups whole milk
1 cup medjool dates, pitted, chopped
¼ cup yellow raisins
¼ cup saffron ghee (page 41)
3 tablespoons extra-virgin olive oil
2 tablespoons honey
1 teaspoon sea salt
1 teaspoon ground cinnamon
½ teaspoon rose water

garnish

Drizzle of organic raw honey
Sprinkle of ground cinnamon

Method

1. Grease a 6-quart nonstick saucepan with 3 tablespoons extra-virgin olive oil. Place rice, 4 cups whole milk, rose water, cinnamon, and salt into the saucepan. With saucepan uncovered, bring to a boil over high heat, reduce heat to medium, and simmer for 20 minutes or until all the milk has been absorbed. Stir occasionally.
2. Once all the milk has absorbed into the rice, add honey, dates, yellow raisins, and drizzle ¼ cup saffron ghee over the rice. Gently fold ingredients together. Warp the lid of the 6-quart nonstick sauté pan in a clean tea towel, and place lid tightly on the pan. Continue cooking over low heat for 25 to 30 minutes.
3. Remove from heat, place pot in a large stainless steel mixing bowl half way filled with ice water (this helps to free the tadig), and let cool for 5 minutes.
4. Once cooled, hold a flat serving platter tightly over the uncovered pot, and invert the cooked rice onto the serving platter (like inverting a cake out of a pan).
5. Serve warm, and garnish with a drizzle of honey, and a sprinkle of ground cinnamon.

variation:

Rose Bud Rice (Gol'e Mohammadi Polo): Follow the above recipe. However, in Step 1 add ¼ cup dried rose pedals that has been soaked in cold water for 5 minutes, and drained. Continue to follow instructions as directed.

persian sticky rice
kateh

This is a very classic recipe from Northern Iran by the Caspian Sea. Unlike most Persian rice dishes kateh is a sticky simple rice cooked in one saucepan. This rice is so easy to make, and has such a rich flavor thanks to the ghee. serves 6

Ingredients For Rice

2 cups long-grain basmati rice,
soaked in water for 2 hours, rinsed,
drained
4 cups water
¼ cup saffron ghee
3 tablespoons extra-virgin olive oil
2 tablespoons sea salt

Method

1. Grease a 6-quart nonstick saucepan with 3 tablespoons extra-virgin olive oil. Place rice, 4 cups water, and salt into the saucepan. With saucepan uncovered, bring to a boil over high heat, reduce heat to medium, and simmer for 20 minutes or until all the water has been absorbed. Stir occasionally.

2. Once all the water has absorbed into the rice, drizzle ¼ cup saffron ghee over the rice. Warp the lid of the 6-quart nonstick sauté pan in a clean tea towel, and place lid tightly on the pan. Continue cooking over low heat for 25 to 30 minutes.

3. Remove from heat, place pot in a large stainless steel mixing bowl half way filled with ice water (this helps to free the tadig), and let cool for 5 minutes.

4. Once cooled, hold a flat serving platter tightly over the uncovered pot, and invert the cooked rice onto the serving platter (like inverting a cake out of a pan).

5. Serve warm with any kind of khoresh (stew), or yogurt.

baked saffron yogurt rice with chicken — tachin-e morgh

This rice and chicken recipe is so easy to make there's no need for too much explanation. It's one of those dishes that come to the rescue when you have limited time and ingredients but are looking for a simple, warm, and satisfying meal to round off your day. *serves 6*

Ingredients For Rice

1 ½ pound skinless chicken breast, cut into 1 ½ pieces
2 cups long-grain basmati rice, soaked in water for 2 hours, rinsed, drained
4 cups water
1 cup plain yogurt
1 medium yellow onion, finely sliced
1 tablespoon turmeric
2 tablespoons sea salt
Pinch of saffron threads (grinded & dissolved in 2 tablespoons hot water)
2 tablespoons extra-virgin olive oil

Ingredients For Crust

(Tadig)
1 cup plain yogurt
4 egg yolks
Pinch of saffron threads (grinded & dissolved in 2 tablespoons hot water)

garnish
1 cup barberries, cleaned
¼ cup saffron ghee
½ cup slivered pistachios, soaked in water for 1 hour, drained
2 tablespoons granulated sugar
2 tablespoons rose water

Method

1. In a medium mixing bowl place chicken, 1 cup yogurt, onions, turmeric, saffron liquid, and mix ingredients together. Cover, and let marinate in the refrigerator for 2 to 4 hour.
2. Remove chicken from the marinade (reserving marinade liquid). In medium sauté pan drizzle extra-virgin olive oil, and place chicken sauté over medium heat for 7 minutes.
3. In a 6-quart saucepan place 4 cups water, and salt. Bring to a boil over high heat. Once at a boil pour drained rice, and 2 tablespoons extra-virgin olive oil into the saucepan. Boil briskly for exactly 5 minutes, drain rice in a large, fine-mesh colander and risen with cold water. Set Aside.
4. Adjust oven rack to the middle position, and preheat oven to 375° F.
5. In a medium-mixing bowl place 1 cup parboiled rice, 1 cup yogurt, 4 egg yolks, 2 teaspoons saffron liquid, and mix ingredients together. Spread the mixture onto the bottom of a well-buttered 9-inch nonstick pan. Pour half the parboiled rice into the pan and flatten with a spoon. Then place chicken pieces on top and flatten. Pour in the rest of the parboiled rice into the pan and firmly flatten again. Drizzle rice with the reserved chicken marinade.
6. Cover pan with aluminum foil and bake for 2 hours
7. In a nonstick sauté pan, place ¼ cup saffron ghee, barberries, sultanas, pistachios, 4 tablespoons of sugar, and 2 tablespoons rose water. Sauté for 1 minute, while stirring constantly (barberries burn quickly), remove from heat, and set aside.
8. Remove from pan from oven, place pan in a large stainless steel mixing bowl half way filled ice (this helps to free the tadig), and let cool for 5 minutes.
9. Once cooled, hold a flat serving platter tightly over the uncovered pan, and invert the cooked rice onto the serving platter (like inverting a cake out of a pan).
10. Serve warm, and garnish with barberries mixture atop.

rice with brown lentils, raisins and dates ~ addas polo

This is a perfect rice dish to serve to a vegetarian guest. The rice, brown lentil, raisins, and dates provide a full-throttle sweet and savory dish filled with taste and texture that marriages beautifully together. *serves 6*

Ingredients For Rice

4 cups long-grain basmati rice, soaked in water for 2 hours, rinsed, drained
1 cup brown lentils, soaked for 2 hours, drained
¼ cup saffron ghee (page 41),
1 teaspoon turmeric
1 teaspoon cinnamon
Pinch of saffron threads (grinded & dissolved in 2 tablespoons hot water)
1 tablespoon salt
Drizzle of extra-virgin olive oil

For the raisin & date mixture:

1 yellow onion, thinly sliced
a drizzle of extra-virgin olive oil
½ teaspoon cinnamon
12 Majdoul dates, pitted
¼ cup raisins

Ingredients For Crust

(Tadig)

¼ cup saffron ghee (see page 41)
2 egg yolks
Pinch of saffron threads (grinded & dissolved in 2 tablespoons hot water)

Method

1. For the raisin & Date Mixture: In a medium nonstick sauté pan drizzle extra-virgin olive oil, place onions, cinnamon and sauté onions until golden. Add pitted dates, and raisins, stir constantly and sauté for 4-5 minutes, until dates and raisins puff up. Remove from heat set aside.

2. In a 4-quart saucepan place 2 cups water, and bring to a boil over medium heat. Add brown lentils and cook for 15-25 minutes until they are just soft , and not falling apart. Remove from, drain, and set aside.

3. In a 6-quart saucepan place 8 cups water, turmeric, and salt. Bring to a boil over high heat. Once at a boil place rice, and a drizzle 2 oft extra-virgin olive oil into the saucepan. Boil for exactly 10 minutes, drain rice in a large, fine-mesh colander, and risen with cold water. Set Aside.

4. Next on the bottom of a medium nonstick sauté pan place ¼ cup saffron ghee in sauté pan, and spread saffron ghee over the enter bottom of the pan. Place 2 spatulas of the parboiled rice-lentil mixture into the pan, then place 1 spatula of Raisin date mixture distributing it evenly on top of the rice. Repeat these steps, while gradually arranging the rice into the shape of a pyramid. Drizzle the remaining saffron ghee, and the saffron liquid over the rice.

5. Warp the lid of the nonstick sauté pan in a clean tea towel, and place lid tightly on the pan. Steam over medium heat for 30 to 35 minutes.

6. Place rice on a serving platter, and arrange crust (tadig) around the rice platter.

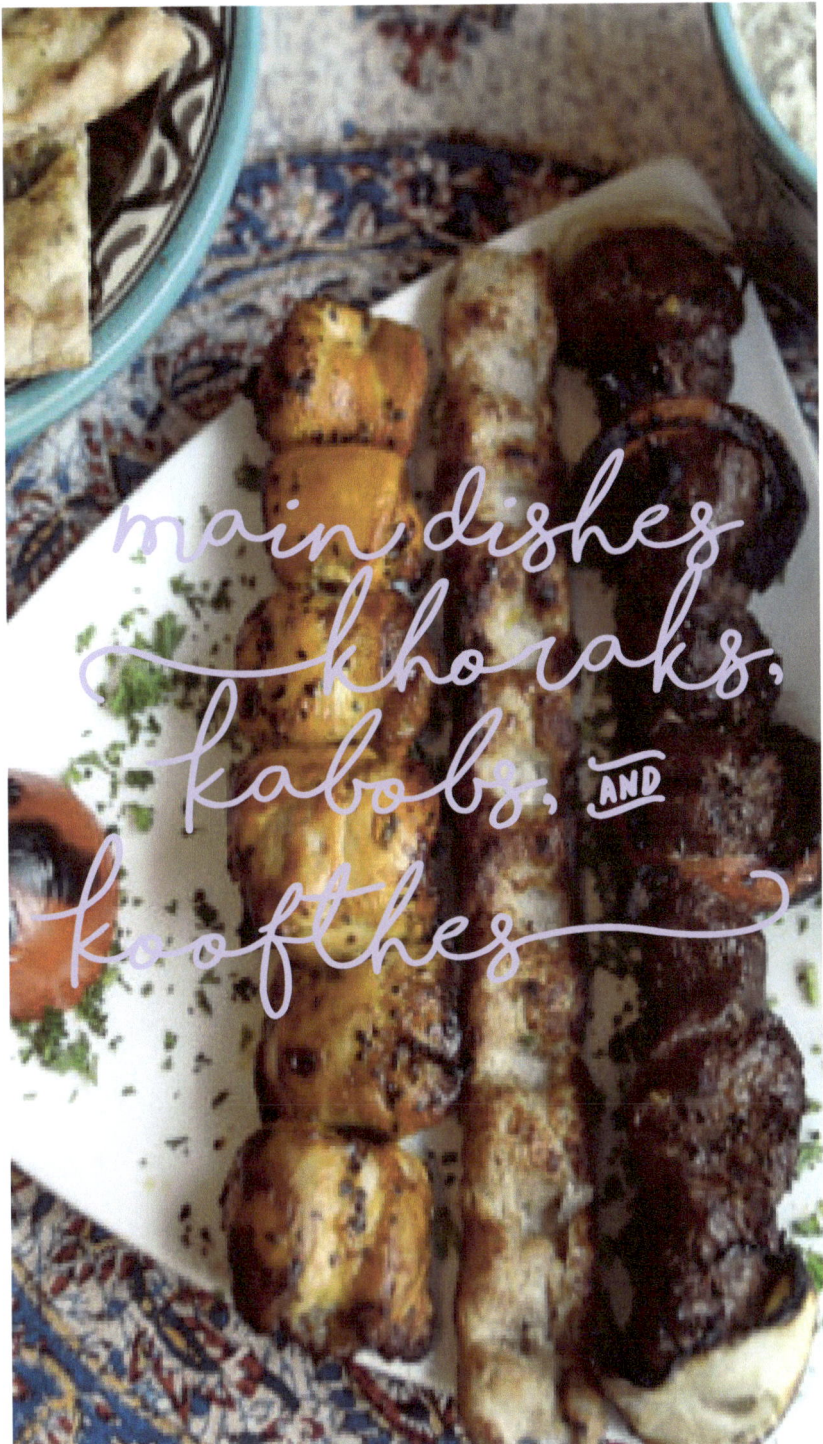

main dishes
khoraks,
kabobs, and
kooftehs

Persians are quite fond of red meats and have a variety of ways for preparing it: kababs, koofteh, and dolmeh. Traditionally lamb is the red meat of choice in Iran. Nevertheless beef can be substituted.

Kababs are pieces of meat marinated, and skewered on long metal skewers and grilled on a hot barbecue. When preparing kababs marinate the meat for at least 5 hours. 8 hours is preferred, so that the meat absorbs the flavors and aromas of the ingredients used in the marinade.

Koofteh are meatballs and are an old Persian dish that originates from Tabriz the capital of East Azerbayan Province of Iran.

Dolmeh are vegetables or fruits stuffed with a mixture or rice, aromatic spices and meat.

Please note: before serving cooked meat, allow cooked meat to rest for 5-10 minutes so that juices and flavors can redistribute.

fillet kabob ~ kababe barg

Succulent strips of fillet mignon, or lamb tenderloin marinated in a lemon saffron sauce, Pounded flat like a leaf (barg), and grilled on a skewer to perfection. *serves 4*

Ingredients For Marinad
2 pounds lean tenderloin steak
(preferably fillet mignon)
1 cups onion juice (2 onions, peeled, pureed and strained)
½ cup extra-virgin olive oil
¼ cup fresh lemon juice
Pinch of saffron threads (grinded & dissolved in 2 tablespoons water)
2 tablespoons sumac
1 tablespoon garlic powder
1 teaspoon freshly ground black pepper
1 teaspoon sea salt

Baste
¼ cup saffron ghee
Pinch of saffron threads (grinded & dissolved in 2 tablespoons water)
½ teaspoon sea salt
½ teaspoon freshly ground black pepper

garnish & supplies
4 flat ¾ inch wide stainless steel skewers
6 pieces of fresh lavish bread
4 medium heirloom tomatoes

Method

1. Cut meat into ¼ inch thick strips, against the grain on a diagonal. Place meat into a large mixing bowl. Add onion juice, extra-virgin olive oil, lemon juice, saffron liquid, sumac, garlic powder, black pepper, and salt. Thoroughly incorporate all ingredients together. Cover bowl, and marinate for 24 hours in the refrigerator.
2. Thread each piece of meat onto the stainless steel skewer, leaving a few inches free on both sides of the skewer. Using the flat side of a meat mallet, pond the edges of the meat to create a straight line on both sides. Spear the tomatoes on separate skewers.
3. Preheat an outdoor or indoor grill to medium-high heat.
4. In a medium sauté pan, place saffron ghee, saffron liquid, sea salt, and freshly ground black pepper. Heat over medium heat for 5 minutes.
5. Place tomatoes on the grill, and brush lightly with baste mixture. Grill tomatoes for 15-20 minutes, while rotating the sewer every 5 minutes.
6. Baste meat skewers on both sides, arrange skewers on the grill, and cook for 2-4 minutes on each side (while basting and rotating the skewers frequently).
7. Remove the skewers form the grill, baste, and place on a platter covered in lavash. Sprinkle kabob with sumac powder.

variation:

Rice with kabob (Chelo Kabob): Chelo Kabob is the national dish of Iran. Chelo kabob is traditionally made with lamb fillet, and served with white rice (Chelo), topped with butter, adorned atop with egg yolk, and a generous sprinkle of sumac. To serve chelow kabob: Place a mound of chelo (see page 92) in a plate, make a small hole in the center of the rice, and place the yolk of one egg. Add a nob of butter to the rice, and sprinkle rice with sumac. Place kabobs, grilled tomatoes on the side of the rice, and serve with yogurt and lightly grilled onions.

ground meat kabob ~ kababe koobideh

Succulent strips of fillet mignon, or lamb tenderloin marinated in a lemon saffron sauce, Pounded flat like a leaf (barg), and grilled on a skewer to perfection. *serves 4-6*

Ingredients For Marinad:

2 pounds ground beef, or ground lamb
1 large yellow onion, peeled, rinsed, finely grated, strained
3 tablespoons crushed breadcrumbs
Pinch of saffron threads (grinded & dissolved in 2 tablespoons water)
1 egg yolk
2 tablespoons sumac
1 tablespoon garlic powder
1 teaspoon freshly ground black pepper
1 teaspoon turmeric
1 teaspoon ground cinnamon
½ teaspoon sea salt

Baste

¼ cup fresh lemon juice
½ teaspoon sea salt
½ teaspoon freshly ground black pepper

garnish & supplies

8 flat ¾ inch wide stainless steel skewers
6 pieces of fresh lavish bread
2 large heirloom tomatoes, halved vertically
2 medium white onions, halved vertically

Method

1. Place ground meat into a large mixing bowl. Add strained onions, crushed breadcrumbs, saffron liquid, egg yolk, sumac, garlic powder, black pepper, turmeric, ground cinnamon, and salt. Thoroughly incorporate all ingredients together. Cover bowl, and marinate for 24 hours in the refrigerator.

2. Preheat an outdoor or indoor grill to high heat.

3. With damp hands, divide the meat mixture into 12 balls the size of a tangerine.
Pierce the meat with the stainless steel skewer, and slide the meat down to the middle of the skewer. Gently squeeze meat around the skewer to form a log-shaped kabob. Softly indent the meat skewer every ½ inch by using two fingers, and create ridges along the meat. Repeat until all meat mixture has been used

4. Spear the tomatoes, onions, and serrano peppers on separate skewers.

5. In a medium mixing bowl, place lemon juice, sea salt, freshly ground black pepper, and whisk ingredients together.

6. Place tomatoes, onions, serrano peppers on the grill, and brush ingredients lightly with baste mixture. Grill for 15 minutes, while rotating the sewers every 5 minutes.

7. Baste meat skewers on both sides, arrange skewers on the grill, and cook for 2-4 minutes on each side (while basting and rotating the skewers frequently).

8. Remove the skewers form the grill, baste, and place on a platter covered in lavash.

9. Serve with chelo (saffron steamed rice).

tender beef braised with cinnamon and prunes
tas kabab

This dish is traditionally made in a Gamaj, however they are hard to find in the west so instead I used a medium-large tagine, and it works out lovely. *serves 4-6*

Ingredients

Drizzle of Extra-virgin olive oil
1 ½ ponds stew meat beef, or lamb cut into 2-inch cubes
1 cup prunes, pitted
2 white, or yellow onions, thinly sliced
2 garlic cloves, finely minced
4 carrots, peeled, finely cut into ½-inch discs
2 large potatoes, peeled, cut into small cubes
2 tomatoes, thickly sliced
1 teaspoon turmeric
1 teaspoon ground cinnamon
1 teaspoon sea salt
½ teaspoon fresh ground black pepper
¼ cup fresh lemon juice
4 tablespoons tomato paste
Pinch of saffron threads (grinded & dissolved in 2 tablespoons hot water)

Method

1. In a Gamaj or medium-large Tagine drizzle extra-virgin olive oil. Next layer the pan with the sliced onions, then add a layer of meat, following separate layers of tomatoes, carrots, while sprinkling each layer with ground cinnamon, turmeric, salt, and freshly ground pepper. Top the layers with the pitted prunes.

2. In a small mixing bowl place lemon juice, and tomato paste, and whisk ingredients together. Pour mixture into the gamaj, and drizzle with extra-virgin olive oil.

3. Cover, and cook for 15 minutes. Reduce heat to low and cook for 45-50 minutes, until meat is tender. Add Saffron liquid 5 minutes before serving.

4. Serve warm accompanied by chelo (Steamed rice).

tabriz meatballs — koofteh tabrizi

This is a lovely and filling dish, spiced meatballs stuffed with a hard boiled egg, and braised in a piquant tomato base. This dish is form Tabriz where they are famous for making the best Koofteh (meatballs). serves 4-6

Ingredients For Meatballs
1 pond ground beef or lamb
½ cup chickpea powder
1 large yellow onion, peeled, grated
Pinch of saffron threads (grinded & dissolved in 2 tablespoons water)
1 teaspoon sea salt
1 teaspoon ground black pepper
1 teaspoon cinnamon
1 teaspoon nutmeg
½ teaspoon turmeric
2 egg yolks

Filling
4 eggs, hard-boiled, de-shelled
8 golden dried plums (Alu Zard), pitted
Drizzle of extra-virgin olive oil

Broth
5 cups vegetable broth
2 lemons, juiced
4 tablespoons tomato paste
1 teaspoon turmeric

Method

1. Adjust oven rack to the middle position, and preheat oven to 350° F.
2. In a large mixing bowl place ground meat, chickpea powder, grated onions, and thoroughly mix ingredients together. Add saffron liquid, salt, pepper, cinnamon, nutmeg, turmeric, egg yolks, and mix well.
3. Shape the meat mixture into four large balls of equal size. Make a hole in the center of each meatball; and place 1 hard-boiled egg, 2 golden plums. Cover hole with meat mixture, Seal, and smooth the outside of the meatballs. Continue until all mixture is used, place each meatball onto a well-buttered baking dish.
4. In a medium saucepan, drizzle extra-virgin olive oil, add 4 cups vegetable broth, lemon juice, tomato paste, and turmeric. Let simmer over medium heat for 10 minutes.
5. Pour broth around the meatballs. Cover baking dish with aluminum foil and transfer to oven; bake for 35 minutes. Uncover pan, rotate meatballs, and baste meatballs with juice from the pan. Continue cooking for 10 more minutes.
6. Place Meatballs on a serving tray, serve hot accompanied by Mast-e kisseh (thick yogurt).

110

stuffed quince ～ dolmehiye beh

Stuffed quince's is one of my family's favorite autumn treats.
serves 4-6

Ingredients

6 medium-sized quinces,
1 pond ground beef or lamb
½ cup rice, soaked for 2 hours
¼ cup honey
1 medium yellow onion, peeled, grated
4 tablespoons tomato paste
2 tablespoons extra-virgin olive oil
Pinch of saffron threads (grinded &
dissolved in 2 tablespoons water)
1 teaspoon sea salt
½ teaspoon cinnamon
½ teaspoon nutmeg
½ teasoon turmeric
½ teaspoon cayenne powder
1 egg yolk

Broth

4 cups vegetable broth
¼ cup lemon juice
¼ cup honey
Pinch of saffron threads (grinded &
dissolved in 2 tablespoons water)

Method

1. Wash and rub the fuzz off the quinces. Cut of the tops of the quinces, and set aside. Hollow out the quinces very carefully using a melon baller. Make sure to remove all seeds. Make sure to reserve pulp.

2. In a 6-quart saucepan place 4 cups water, and salt. Bring to a boil over high heat. Once at a boil pour drained rice, and 2 tablespoons extra-virgin olive oil into the saucepan. Boil briskly for exactly 5 minutes, drain rice in a large, fine-mesh colander and risen with cold water. Set Aside.

3. In a large mixing bowl place ground meat, grated onions, and thoroughly mix ingredients together. Add saffron liquid, cinnamon, nutmeg, turmeric, cayenne, egg yolks, and mix well.

4. Stuff quinces with meat mixture, and place lids on the quinces. Place quinces upright in a deep saucepan, and add the reserved pulp around the quinces. Pour in the saucepan vegetable broth, lemon juice, honey and saffron liquid. Cook over medium heat for 10 minutes, then reduce heat to low and cook for 45 minutes, or until the quinces are tender.

5. To serve, place quinces in a serving dish, pour pan juices over quinces. Serve with yogurt accompanied by fresh herbs.

stuffed cabbage leaves
dolmehiye kalam

Stuffed savoy cabbage leaves with Beef and spices. Serve these bundles of joy yogurt for a comforting winter meal. *serves 4-6*

Ingredients:

2 large head of green or savory cabbage
1 ½ pond ground beef or lamb
2 carrots, peeled, shredded
½ cup cooked rice
1 medium yellow onion, peeled, grated
4 tablespoons tomato paste
Pinch of saffron threads (grinded & dissolved in 2 tablespoons water)
¼ cup fresh flat-leaf parsley, roughly chopped
1 teaspoon turmeric
½ teaspoon ground cinnamon
½ teaspoon freshly ground black pepper
½ teaspoon sea salt
drizzle of extra-virgin olive oil
2 quarts water

Broth

2 carrots, peeled, shredded
5 cups fresh tomato puree

Method

1. Core cabbage using a paring knife, and carefully remove individual leaves. Place 2 quarts water into a 6-qaurt saucepan, and bring to a boil over medium-high heat. Add cabbage leaves and cook for 5 minutes, or until outer leaves are tender. Drain leaves in a colander, and leave to cool. Trim thick center vein from bottom of each leaf. Reserve four large outer leaves to line bottom of pan, and 4 leaves to cover the Stuffed Cabbages.

2. In a large mixing bowl place ground meat, carrots, onions, cooked rice, tomato paste, saffron liquid, parsley, black pepper, sea salt, and mix ingredients together.

3. To stuff the cabbage leaves, place 2 tablespoons meat mixture 1 inch above the steam of the leaf. Fold both sides of the cabbage over filling, and starting with the stem end, roll the cabbage up. Repeat this process with remaining leaves and filling.

4. Line a 5-quart Dutch oven with the 4 reserved cabbage leaves. Transfer stuffed cabbage leaves to Dutch oven, placing them steam side down.

5. Pour tomato puree over cabbage (make sure all cabbage rolls are covered with puree), sprinkle stuffed cabbage with shredded carrots, and cover with the remaining reserved cabbage leaves.

6. Bring Dutch oven to a boil, and reduce heat to low. Cover Dutch oven and cook for 45 minutes, adding additional tomato puree as needed.

7. To serve, place stuffed cabbage in a serving dish, pour sauce over stuffed cabbage, and serve hot accompanied by Mast'e kisseh (thick yogurt).

chicken fillet kabob — kababie morghie barg

This is a Fine chicken breast kaoab marinated in a lemon yogurt-saffron sauce that is pounded flat like a leaf (barg), and grilled on a skewer to perfection. *serves 4-6*

Ingredients For Marinad:
3 pounds skinless, boneless, chicken breast
1 cup onion juice (2 onions, peeled, pureed and strained)
½ cup extra-virgin olive oil
1 cup fresh lemon juice
½ cup plain yogurt
½ cup fresh orange juice
½ cup fresh flat-leaf parsley
Pinch of saffron threads (grinded & dissolved in 2 tablespoons hot water)
1 tablespoon garlic powder
1 teaspoon turmeric
1 teaspoon freshly ground black pepper
1 teaspoon sea salt

Baste
½ cup fresh lemon juice
½ cup fresh orange juice
Pinch of saffron threads (grinded & dissolved in 2 tablespoons hot water)
½ teaspoon sea salt
½ teaspoon freshly ground black pepper

garnish & supplies
4 flat ¾ inch wide stainless steel skewers
6 pieces of fresh lavish bread
4 medium heirloom tomatoes

Method

1. Cut chicken into ¼ inch thick strips, against the grain on a diagonal. Place chicken into a large mixing bowl. Add onion juice, extra-virgin olive oil, lemon juice, yogurt, orange juice, flat-leaf parsley, saffron liquid, garlic powder, black pepper, and salt. Thoroughly incorporate all ingredients together. Cover bowl, and marinate for 24 hours in the refrigerator.
2. Thread each piece of chicken onto the stainless steel skewer, leaving a few inches free on both sides of the skewer. Using the flat side of a meat mallet, and pond the edges of the chicken to create a straight line on both sides. Spear the tomatoes on separate skewers.
3. Preheat an outdoor or indoor grill to medium-high heat.
4. In a large mixing bowl place lemon juice, orange juice, saffron liquid, sea salt, and freshly ground black pepper, and whisk ingredients together.
5. Place tomatoes on the grill, and brush lightly with baste mixture. Grill tomatoes for 15-20 minutes, while rotating the sewer every 5 minutes.
6. Baste chicken skewers on both sides, arrange skewers on the grill, and cook for 3-5 minutes on each side (while basting and rotating the skewers frequently).
7. Remove the skewers form the grill, baste, and place on a platter covered in lavash.
8. Serve with chelo (saffron steamed rice).

chicken kabob ~ joojeh kabab

This is a Fine chicken breast kaoab marinated in a lemon-yogurt-saffron sauce that is pounded flat like a leaf (barg), and grilled on a skewer to perfection. *serves 4-6*

Ingredients For Marinad:

3 pounds skinless, boneless, chicken breast, cut into 2 inch cubes
1 cup onion juice (2 onions, peeled, pureed and strained)
½ cup fresh cilantro, roughly chopped
1 cup non-alcoholic white wine
1 cup fresh lemon juice
¼ cup extra-virgin olive oil
Pinch of saffron threads (grinded & dissolved in 2 tablespoons hot water)
1 tablespoon garlic powder
1 teaspoon freshly ground black pepper
1 teaspoon sea salt

Baste

½ cup non-alcoholic white wine
½ cup fresh lemon juice
½ teaspoon sea salt
½ teaspoon freshly ground black pepper

garnish and supplies

9 flat ¼ inch wide stainless steel skewers
2 large heirloom tomatoes, halved vertically
2 medium white onions, halved vertically
6 green Serrano peppers

Method

1. Place chicken into a large mixing bowl. Add onion juice, cilantro, non-alcoholic white wine, lemon juice, extra-virgin olive oil, saffron liquid, garlic powder, black pepper, and salt. Thoroughly incorporate all ingredients together. Cover bowl, and marinate for 24 hours in the refrigerator.

2. Preheat an outdoor or indoor grill to medium-high heat.

3. In a medium mixing bowl, place non-alcoholic white wine, lemon juice, salt, freshly ground black pepper, and whisk ingredients together.

4. Drain meat and discard of marinade. Using 6 stainless steel skewers, thread meat on skewers.

5. Spear the tomatoes, onions, and serrano peppers on separate skewers.

6. Place skewers on grill and cook for 8-10 minutes on each side, or until chicken reaches desired doneness (while basting the skewers frequently).

7. Remove the skewers form the grill, drizzle kebobs with baste, and serve with chelo (saffron steamed rice).

114

roasted chicken stuffed with apricots, and prunes ~ morghe shekampor

This dish just looks so beautiful, especially when you carve it at the table, and it taste simply majestic. Serve on the side with the stuffing for a pure decadent dining experience. This dish is a showstopper, so next time you have guests, why don't you dazzle them with this delicious meal. serves 4-6

Ingredients :

1 chicken (about 6 ponds), remove giblets, rinse chicken in cold water
1 yellow onion, chopped
1 stick of butter
½ cup long-grain basmati rice, cooked
½ cup dried apricots
½ cups golden dried plums (Alu Zard), pitted
¼ cup dried tart cherries
½ cup fresh cilantro, roughly chopped
teaspoon turmeric
1 teaspoon paprika
1 teaspoon sea salt
½ teaspoon freshly ground black pepper

baste and garnish

1 cup water
1 whole lemon, cut into ¼ inch slices
1 cup fresh lemon juice
Pinch of saffron threads (grinded & dissolved in 2 tablespoons hot water)
4 lemons, halved

Method

1. Adjust oven rack to the middle position, and preheat oven to 400° F.
2. In a small mixing bowl place turmeric, paprika, sea salt, black pepper, and mix ingredients together. Rub the chicken with ½ stick of butter inside, and outside. Rub the spice mixture over the outside of the chicken.
3. In a medium sauté pan place, onions, ½ stick of butter, and sauté over medium heat until onions turn golden. Add dried apricots, golden dried plums, dried tart cherries, and sauté for 1 minute. Remove from heat, and stir in rice, and cilantro to mixture. Set aside.
4. Place the chicken on a roasting rack in a roasting pan. Pour ½ cup lemon juice inside the cavity of the chicken, and stuff chicken with the fruit mixture. Sew or pin the chicken cavity shut. Using a loop of kitchen string, tie the wings to the sides of the chicken, and tie the ends of the drumsticks together.
5. Arrange lemon slices on top of the chicken. Add ½ cup water to the pan. Roast for 1 ½, or until an instant-read thermometer inserted in the thickest part of the thigh (not touching any bones) reads 170° F. Make sure to baste the chicken with pan juices every 30 minutes.
6. Remove chicken form oven, and let stand at room temperature for 15 minutes. Pour the pan juices into a gravy separator, let stand for 5 minutes, pour off the drippings, and discard the fat.
7. Place chicken on a serving tray, and pour gravy into a sauceboat. Garnish the chicken with lemon halves, and fresh herbs.

chicken braised with yogurt and olives ~ morghe mast ba zaytoon

This is one of those recipes you just can't make once: once you make it you'll be hooked. The yogurt and olives in this dish adds a luxurious accompaniment to the tender, but not strongly flavored, chicken. serves 4-6

Ingredients

Drizzle of Extra-virgin olive oil
8 Skinned chicken legs
1 cup green olives, pitted
1 ½ cup yogurt
½ cup fresh lemon juice
2 white, or yellow onions, thinly sliced
½ cup fresh parsley, finely chopped
½ cup fresh cilantro, finely chopped
2 garlic cloves, finely minced
1 teaspoon turmeric
1 teaspoon ground cumin
1 teaspoon Paprika
1 teaspoon sea salt
½ teaspoon fresh ground black pepper
Pinch of saffron threads (grinded & dissolved in 2 tablespoons hot water)

Method

1. In a large mixing bowl place: chicken legs, olives, yogurt, onions, chopped parsley, chopped cilantro, minced cloves, turmeric, ground cumin, paprika, salt and pepper. Mix ingredients together until fully incorporated. Cover bowl, and marinate for 4 hours in the refrigerator.

2. Adjust oven rack to the middle position, and preheat oven to 325° F.

3. In a Gamaj or medium-large Tagine drizzle extra-virgin olive oil. Place chicken mixture into the Gamaj, Cover, and cook for 15 minutes over medium heat. Reduce heat to low and cook for 25 minutes, until meat is tender. Add Saffron liquid 5 minutes before serving.

4. Serve warm accompanied by chelo (Steamed rice).

salmon kabob — kababie mahi

When you don't have the time to marinate overnight this salmon kabab recipe is perfect. In fact, at all times, constraints or not, this dish is perfect to make especially for entertaining - it is simply gorgeous and delicious. serves 4-6

Ingredients For Marinad

1 skinless salmon fillet (about 2 lbs), cut into 2 inch cubes
1 cup onion juice (2 onions, peeled, pureed and strained)
½ cup fresh cilantro, roughly chopped
1 cup fresh lemon juice
¼ cup extra-virgin olive oil
Pinch of saffron threads (grinded & dissolved in 2 tablespoons hot water)
1 tablespoon garlic powder
1 teaspoon freshly ground black pepper
1 teaspoon sea salt

Baste

1 cup fresh flat-leaf parsley, roughly chopped
1 cup fresh cilantro, roughly chopped
½ cup fresh lemon juice
¼ cup extra-virgin olive oil
2 garlic cloves, peeled
¾ teaspoon crushed red pepper

garnish & supplies

6 flat ¼ inch wide stainless steel skewers
2 medium yellow onions, cut into 1-inch wedges
1 large green pepper, deseeded, cut into 1-inch wedges
1 large sweet red pepper, deseeded, cut into 1-inch wedges

Method

1. Place fish into a large mixing bowl. Add onion juice, cilantro, lemon juice, extra-virgin olive oil, saffron emulsion, garlic powder, black pepper, and salt. Thoroughly incorporate all ingredients together. Cover bowl, and marinate for 4 hours in the refrigerator.

2. Preheat an outdoor or indoor grill to medium-high heat.

3. In a food processor place flat-leaf parsley, cilantro, lemon juice, extra-virgin olive oil, garlic cloves, crushed red pepper, and blend ingredients for 1 minute. Pour mixture into a small bowl.

4. Drain fish and discard marinade3. Using 6 stainless steel skewers, alternately thread fish and vegetables on skewers.

5. Brush kabobs with base. Place skewers on grill and cook for 5-7 minutes on each side, or until fish reaches desired doneness (while basting the skewers frequently).

6. Remove the skewers form the grill, drizzle kebobs with baste, and serve with yogurt.

117

tamarind infused stuffed red snapper — mahi'e shekampor

A dash of cayenne pepper in this dish gives it a little kick. This dish is gloriously easy: you just season and stuff the red snapper and place it in a baking sheet and leave it to cook in the oven until flesh flakes easily with a fork. *serves 4-6*

Ingredients For Marinad

1 whole red snapper (about 2.5 pounds), scaled, rinsed inside and out, pat dry with a paper towel
1 teaspoon sea salt
1 teaspoon turmeric
½ teaspoon powdered dried lime
¾ ground cayenne pepper

Stuffing

1 cup fresh flat-leaf parsley, roughly chopped
1 cup fresh cilantro, roughly chopped
½ stick butter
¼ cup lemon vest
4 garlic cloves, peeled, minced
½ cup dried tart cherries, soaked in water for 10 minutes, drained
two tablespoons tamarind paste
¾ teaspoon crushed red pepper

Baste

1 cup fresh lemon juice

Method

1. Adjust oven rack to the middle position, and preheat oven to 400° F.

2. In a small mixing bowl place turmeric, sea salt, powdered dried lime, cayenne pepper and mix ingredients together. Rub the spice mixture over the inside, and outside of the fish

3. In a medium sauté pan place ½ stick of butter, lemon vest, garlic, tamarind paste, red pepper, and sauté over medium heat for 1 minute. Add dried tart cherries, and sauté for 1 another minute. Remove from heat, and stir in flat-leaf parsley, and cilantro to mixture. Set aside.

4. Place the fish on a backing sheet lined with aluminum foil. Stuff the cavity of the fish with herb mixture, and pin the fish cavity shut with toothpicks.

5. Pour lemon juice over fish, and bake uncovered for 30 minutes, or until flesh flakes easily with a fork.

6. Transfer the fish to a serving platter, discard toothpicks, and serve with rice.

halibut braised in pomegranate and orange juice — mahi ba db'e mir eh

This is a special dish, it's something light, sweet, savory and out of the ordinary that I make for special occasions. The savory and sweet combination of luscious pomegranate and orange juice creates a delight decadent fillet of halibut. It's such a beautiful dish to serve that I love garnishing the fillets with thinly sliced rings of orange – pure flavor bliss. *serves 4-6*

Ingredients For Marinad

4 skinless halibut fillets (6 ounces each)
½ cup butter, melted butter
½ cup fresh pomegranate juice
½ cup fresh orange juice
½ teaspoon ground cinnamon
¼ teaspoon grated nutmeg
¼ teaspoon ground cloves
Pinch of salt
Pinch of freshly ground black pepper

garnish

1 orange, thinly sliced into rings

Method

1. In a Large mixing bowl place butter, pomegranate juice, orange juice, ground cinnamon, grated nutmeg, ground cloves, salt, and freshly ground pepper. Whisk ingredients together until incorporated. Place halibut fillets into the mixing bowl and marinate the for 7 minutes.

2. Adjust oven rack to the middle position, and preheat oven to 375° F.

3. Place the fish fillets on a backing sheet lined with aluminum foil, and pour marinate on top. Bake uncovered for 10-12 minutes, or until flesh flakes easily with a fork.

4. Arrange fish fillets on a serving dish, and garnish atop with orange rings.

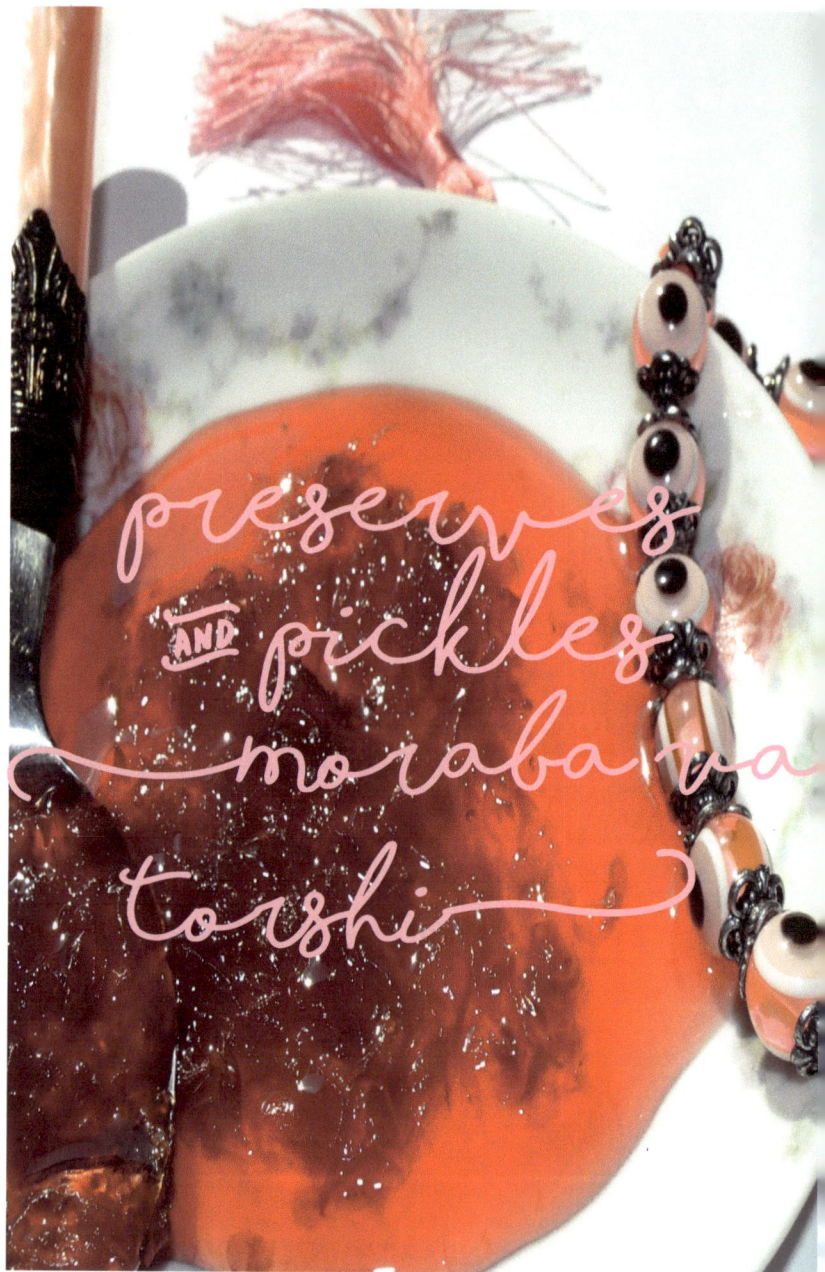

preserves *and* pickles

moraba va torshi

Moraba (preserves) are a staple on the Persian breakfast table, served with warm bread and a knob of butter. A spoon full of preserves are also added to a warm cup of tea for additional flavor & sweetness.

Torshi (pickles) are an indispensable part of Persian food culture, as Persians believe in accordance with Unani that fermented foods are beneficial for a healthy gut and overall well being. With this being said Persians love to pickle everything from garlic to grapes. There are literally endless options of making torshi, and within each region of Iran there are different versions according to local produce and preference.

In the following pages I have included my favorite torshis.

quince preserves — *morabaye beh*

There is a hint of the days-gone-by in this sweet ruby red preserve. Enjoy for breakfast alongside feta cheese and barbari nan (thick Persian bread). This also is a lovely garnished atop of vanilla ice cream. *makes 3 medium size jars*

Ingredients
2 pounds quince
½ teaspoon cardamom powder
½ tsp cinnamon powder
½ cup brown sugar
1 cinnamon stick
2 whole cardamom pods
1 cup water
½ rose water

supplies
3 medium canning jars

Method

1. In a 6-quart saucepan boil water, and place canning jars, seals and lids into the water to be sterilize, drain and allow to dry.

2. Peel quince, cut each one in half and scoop out seeds.

3. Cut the quinces into 1/2-inch slices, and place in a bowl of cold water as you slice them, to prevent discoloration. Drain quince slices.

4. Place drained quince wedges in a heavy-bottomed medium saucepan on medium heat. Sprinkle with cardamom powder, cinnamon powder and brown sugar.

5. Add the cinnamon stick, cardamom pods, water, and rose water.

6. Cook the preserves for about 2 hours, stirring gently every 25 minutes, or until the liquid is reduced to a thick syrup, and the quinces have turned red. However, the quince wedges should still retain their shape. Remove from heat and allow to cool.

7. Fill the sterilized jars with the mixture, seal and store in a cool dark place.

sour cherry preserves
morabaye albalu

This sour cherry preserve is lovely when spooned into a warm cup of tea. *makes 3 medium size jars*

Ingredients
3 pounds sour cherries
2 cups sugar
4 tablespoons lemon juice

supplies
3 medium canning jars

Method

1. In a 6-quart saucepan boil water, and place canning jars, seals and lids into the water to be sterilize, drain and allow to dry.

2. Remove stems from cherries, wash and drain, and pat dry with a towel. Place cherries on a clean cloth, and let cherries dry for 1-2 hours. Gently remove the pits of the cherries with a toothpick.

3. Place cherries, and sugar in a large mixing bowl. Cover the bowl, and refrigerate overnight.

4. Place cherry mixture in a heavy-bottomed medium saucepan on medium heat, and add the lemon juice.

5. Cook the preserves for about 30 minutes, stirring gently every 10 minutes, or until the liquid is reduced to a thick syrup, add the lemon juice and let pan simmer for 5 additional minutes. Remove from heat and allow to cool.

6. Fill the sterilized jars with the mixture, seal and store in a cool dark place.

*Note: If the syrup or compote begins to catch at the bottom of the pan, reduce the heat

rose petal preserves
morabaye gol'e sorkh

This sweet and floral preserve is lovely with bread and warm tea, dollped over yogurt, or served alongside with plain white cake..
makes 3 medium size jars

Ingredients
7 cups pink & red edible,
pesticide-free roses petals
2 cups water
2½ cups sugar
Juice from 2 lemon juice
2 tablespoons rose water

supplies
3 medium canning jars

Method
1. In a 6-quart saucepan pot boil water, and place canning jars, seals and lids into the water to be sterilize, drain and allow to dry.

2. Rinse rose petals, drain with colander, and pat dry petals with a towel. Place dried rose petals in a large mixing bowl, and sprinkle with 1 cup sugar, and the juice from 1 lemon. Cover the bowl, and refrigerate for 5 hour.

3. Place petal mixture in a heavy-bottomed medium saucepan over medium heat, and 2 cups water, and the remanding sugar, and lemon juice.

4. Bring to a boil. And let simmer 15 minutes, stirring gently from time to time.
5. Add rose water and let simmer for 2 minutes. Remove from heat and allow to cool.

6. Fill the sterilized jars with the mixture, seal and store in a cool dark place.

*Note: If the syrup or compote begins to catch at the bottom of the pan, reduce the heat.

mixed pickled vegetables
torshi'e makhlut

An array of different types of pickles are always served alongside any meal be it lunch or dinner. This recipe is an expedited version of pickling so you won't have to wait months to enjoy, you'll only have to wait two days. *makes 3 medium size jars*

Ingredients

5 medium carrots, peeled, rinsed,
angled sliced
2 cups cabbage, washed, roughly cut
into medium squares
1 ½ cup English seedless cucumbers,
rinsed, angle sliced
2 ½ cups white wine vinegar
¼ cup raw honey
4 tablespoons extra-virgin olive oil
1 teaspoon sea salt

supplies

3 medium canning jars

Method

1. In a medium pot boil water, and place canning jars, seals and lids into the water to be sterilize.

2. Place raw honey, extra-virgin olive oil, sea salt and vinegar in a medium-mixing bowl, whisk ingredients together.

3. In a medium saucepan place carrots and sauté with a drizzle of extra-virgin olive oil for 4 minutes over medium heat.

4. In a large mixing bowl place cabbage, carrots, cucumbers, mix ingredients thoroughly. Pour vinegar mixture over vegetables, and stir well.

4. Fill the sterilized jars with the mixture, seal and store for 2 days in a cool dark place.

5. To serve, drain pickled vegetables and toss with fresh mint. Place in serving bowl.

pickled grapes ~ torshiye angoori

Serve this classic Mazandaran (Northern province of Iran) favorite as an accompaniment to a cheese platter, with aside of honeycomb. *makes 3 medium size jars*

Ingredients

2 pounds firm seedless red or
purple grapes
2 ½ cups white wine vinegar
2 tablespoons sea salt
1 cup granulated sugar
1 cinnamon stick
4 whole cloves

supplies

3 medium canning jars

Method

1. In a 6-quart saucepan boil water, and place canning jars, seals and lids into the water to be sterilize, drain and allow to dry thoroughly.

2. Clip the grapes vines into small clusters. Rinse grapes, drain, and pat dry with a towel.

3. Divide the grape clusters among 4 pint-sized sterilized canning jars.

4. In a heavy-bottomed medium saucepan place white wine vinegar, sea salt, granulated sugar, cinnamon stick, and cloves. Bring ingredients to a boil over medium heat, reduce heat to low, and let simmer for 7 minutes. Remove from heat and allow to cool to room temperature.

5. Fill the sterilized jars with the vinegar mixture, seal, and place jars in the refrigerator for at least 12 hours or overnight. Serve cold.

pickled cherries ~ torshiye gilas

These wonderful sweet-and-sour pickled cherries are best enjoyed with an aged cheese, or alongside a piece of chocolate for an unusual tasty flavor combination. *makes 3 medium size jars*

Ingredients
2 pounds Firm sour cherries
2 ½ cups white wine vinegar
1 cup granulated sugar
2 tablespoons sea salt

supplies
3 medium canning jars

Method

1. In a 6-quart saucepan boil water, and place canning jars, seals and lids into the water to be sterilize, drain and allow to dry thoroughly.

2. Leave stems on cherries, wash, drain, and pat dry with a towel. Place cherries on a clean cloth, and let cherries dry for 1-2 hours. Gently remove the pits of the cherries with a toothpick.

3. Divide the cherries among 4 pint-sized sterilized canning jars.

4. In a heavy-bottomed medium saucepan place white wine vinegar, granulated sugar, and sea salt. Bring ingredients to a boil over medium heat, reduce heat to low, and let simmer for 7 minutes. Remove from heat and allow to cool to room temperature.

5. Fill the sterilized jars with the vinegar mixture, seal, and place jars in the refrigerator for at least 48 hours. Serve cold.

Note: should be refrigerated and used within 2 weeks.

pickled garlic — torshiye seer

If you're a garlic lover this recipe is for you. This recipe comes from northern Iran by the Caspian Sea, where they are known for using massive amounts of garlic. Serve as a condiment with meat, or as a mezzeh (appetizer). *makes 3 medium size jars*

Ingredients
1 pound fresh garlic bulbs
4 cups white wine vinegar
8 whole cloves
2 tablespoons honey
2 tablespoons sea salt

supplies
3 medium canning jars

Method

1. In a 6-quart saucepan boil water, and place canning jars, seals and lids into the water to be sterilize, drain and allow to dry thoroughly.

2. Remove the first outer layers of the garlic bulbs. However, while still leaving some skin.

3. Divide the garlic bulbs among 4 pint-sized sterilized canning jars.

4. In a large mixing bowl place: white wine vinegar, honey, sea salt, cloves, and mix ingredients together.

5. Fill the sterilized jars with the vinegar mixture, seal, and store the jars in a cool dark place for at least 4 weeks before eating.

pickled pistachios
torshiye pesteh

I love this flavor combination: these wonderful sweet and tangy pistachios with a hint of spice are simple divine. Serve as an accompaniment to a cheese platter, along with olives. *makes 2 medium size jars*

Ingredients
2 pounds fresh Pistachios
4 cups white wine vinegar
2 tablespoons honey
2 tablespoons sea salt

supplies
2 medium canning jars

Method

1. Remove skin from pistachios, and rinse in cold water, drain, and pat dry with a towel. Place pistachios on a clean cloth, and let pistachios dry for 1-2 hours.

2. In a 6-quart saucepan boil water, and place canning jars, seals and lids into the water to be sterilize, drain and allow to dry thoroughly.

3. Divide the pistachios among 2 pint-sized sterilized canning jars.

4. In a large mixing bowl place: white wine vinegar, honey, sea salt, and mix ingredients together.

5. Fill the sterilized jars with the vinegar mixture, seal, and store the jars in a cool dark place for at least 4 weeks before serving.

hot and cold beverages

nooshabeh

Whenever you enter a Persian home, hospitality plays a major role. Readily available is always a tray adorned with beverages to offer arriving guests. Beverages vary according to season: during the winter its chai (tea), and during the summer its ice-cold sharbats or fresh squeezed juice. Nevertheless, since I'm a tea enthusiast, tea is served all year round even on the hottest of summer days.

For a little more insight, tea is enjoyed all throughout the day and night in small elegant glasses called estkhans. Persians believe that certain teas have different healing properties, and are readily used to treat different ailments.

Sharbats are colorful thirst-quenching beverages made from fruit and floral syrups. I have included the most popular flavors, with this said the flavor combinations and possibilities are endless. Moreover, I encourage you to try whatever flavors tantalize your plate and adapted these recipes to your liking. The sharbat syrups can also be used over crushed ice to make a lovely Persian-infused snow cone.

a proper pot of persian tea
chai

Yes, I am giving you instructions on how to make a proper pot of tea. I know it seems straightforward and easy enough. However, to make a proper pot of tea is truly an art form. Moreover, It's all about timing, to ensure that you don't over steep the tealeaves. As follows are step-by-step instructions on how to brew a proper pot of Persian tea. *6-8 servings depending on dilution*

Ingredients

3 cups cold water
1 heaping tablespoon of Persian black tea

garnish

Sugar cubes (optional)
Rose water (optional)
Rock candy (optional)
Lemon juice (optional)

Method

1. In a teakettle bring water to a boil.

2. Next warm a small teapot by pour a small amount of boiled water from the teakettle, swirl water around, and pour it out.

3. Place tea leaves in the teapot, and fill teapot half way with boiling water. Cover, and Let the tea steep for 5 to 10 minutes. If you are using a samovar, steep the tea on top of the samovar.

4. Serve the tea by filling each glass halfway with tea, and add boiling water from the kettle to dilute the tea to desired strength.

5. Server with your favorite tea compliments.

variation:

Borage Relaxing Herbal Tea (Chai Gol Gavzaban): Chai Gol Gavzaban is a purple flower that grows in the northern part of Iran. The name literally means "cow's tongue flower", and is know for having a calming effect on the nervous system. Readily use this herbal tea to relive stress, and help cure colds. Follow the above recipe. In step 2, substitute the black tea for 2 tablespoons dried borage flowers, and continue to follow the instructions as directed.

Chamomile Tea (Chai Babooneh): Chai Babooneh is used to help settle upset stomachs. This herbal tea is also wonderful as a sleep aid, to help with Insomnia and other sleep disorders. Needless to say this tea should only be consumed during the nighttime. Follow the above recipe. In step 2, substitute the black tea for 4 tablespoons dried chamomile flowers, and continue to follow the instructions as directed.

persian coffee ~ qahveh ~

This strong coffee much like espresso is prepared in an Ibriq: a copper, or brass coffee pot with a long handle, and then poured into small porcelain cups.

In Iran it is a fun pastime to read the coffee grounds, to read: cover the top of your cup with the saucer, and invert the cup and saucer away from yourself using your left hand, and place it upside-down on a table. Let stand undisturbed for 7 minutes. Flip the cup right-side-up and have a family member look for patterns inside the cup (the querent should not read his or her own cup). Patterns such as an apple mean achieving knowledge, palm tree means happiness in love, and so on…

Ingredients

Fine ground Turkish coffee
Sugar
Pinch of ground cardamom
Pinch of saffron
Cold water
Small cups
Albriq (see note below)
Demitasse cups (small cups)

Method

1. Remove skin from pistachios, and rinse in cold water, drain, 1. Start with very cold water. Use The demitasse cup to measure the water needed for each cup of coffee (one demitasse cup of water is about 4 ounces), and pour the water into the Ibriq.

2. For each demitasse cup, add a 1 teaspoon of coffee, along with 1 teaspoon of sugar, Pinch of ground cardamom, and a pinch of saffron.

3. Place the Ibriq on the stove top, mix ingredients together with a small wood spoon, and bring to a boil until the coffee stats to rise over high heat. Immediately remove ibrik from heat before it boils over.

4. Pour Coffee in the demitasse cup along.

Note: Ibriq is a long-handled small pot usually made from copper. They are available for purchase at most Persian or Middle Eastern Markets.

iced coffee
cafe glace

This Lush cold drink is imported from Belgium. Nevertheless, it is considered to be as much a part of Persian culinary culture as Pomegranates and Saffron. This drink is so simple - scarcely a recipe really - but so delicious as a late night, nightcap. *serves 4*

Ingredients
1 1/2 cups cold milk
1 teaspoon sugar
1 cup of brewed instant coffee
4 scoops of vanilla or coffee ice cream
1/2 cup heavy cream, whipped to medium-stiff peaks

Method

1. In a medium saucepan place milk and sugar and bring to a boil over medium heat. Remove saucepan from heat, add coffee, and stir. Allow to cool, and refrigerate for 1 hour.

2. Place two tall freezer safe glasses in the freezer for 30 minutes.

3. Remove glasses from freezer, place two scoops of ice cream in each glass, and pour cold coffee mixture into glasses. Top with whipped cream, and a pinch of chocolate dust.

yogurt soda
doogh

This salty, minty, fizzy, yogurt dink is a refreshing beverage that is always served alongside Kabab. Please note this is a savory and tart drink that is an acquired taste for most. *serves* 4

Ingredients
1½ cups plain yogurt
2 cups sparkling mineral water, or club soda
1 tablespoon of fresh mint finely chopped, or a pinch of dried mint
½ teaspoon salt
¼ teaspoon pepper

garnish
Spring of fresh pint for garnish (optional)

Method

1. Place yogurt, mint, salt, pepper, into a large mixing bowl, gradually adding sparkling mineral water while whisk ingredients together.

2. Pour yogurt mixture into a pitcher, and refrigerate for at least 1 hour before serving.

3. Serve club with ice cubes, and garnish with a spring of mint.

rose water drink
sharbat'e golab

This drink is traditional served cold at Persian weddings, and served warm after a fast. *makes 1 bottle of syrup*

Ingredients
2 cups water
2 cups sugar
½ cup rose water
¼ cup fresh lime juice
¼ cup rosebuds, Wrapped in a bouquet garni

Mixing:
Plain filter water, sparkling water, or club soda
5 Ice cubes per person

garnish
Mint Leaves or rosebuds (optional)

Method

1. In a 4-quart porcelain or enamel saucepan place water and sugar mix ingredients together until sugar has dissolved with a wooden spoon. Bring to a boil, and let simmer for 10 minutes. Stir occasionally with a wooden spoon.

2. Add the lime juice, rose water, rose buds sachet, and cook, uncovered, over medium/low heat for 10 minutes or until light, rose-infused syrup has formed.

3. Remove from heat, set aside to cool. Once cooled use a slotted spoon to remove rose bud sachet from saucepan. Pour the syrup into a clean bottle and cork tightly. Store at room temperature until ready to use.

4. To serve cold mix in a ratio of: 1 part syrup, 3 parts water (or clubs soda), and 5 ice cubes per person. Server Chilled, and garnish with mint leaves and/ or rose buds.

5. To serve warm mix in a ratio of: 1 part syrup, 3 parts warm water. Serve warm.

Note: to make a bouquet garni place rosebuds in a small square peace of muslin, and tie all sides together with kitchen twine.

sharbat'e limoo *lime syrup*

This drink is traditional served cold at Persian weddings, and served warm after a fast. *makes 1 bottle of syrup*

Ingredients
2 cups water
2 cups sugar
½ Fresh Lime juice, or lemon juice
Zest of one lime, or half a lemon

Mixing:
Plain filter water, sparkling water, or club soda
5 Ice cubes per person

garnish
Lime slices (optional)
Spring of fresh mint (optional)

Method

1. In a 4-quart porcelain or enamel saucepan place water and sugar, mix ingredients together until sugar has dissolved with a wooden spoon. Bring to a boil, and let simmer for 10 minutes. Stir occasionally with a wooden spoon.

2. Add the lime juice, lime zest, and cook, uncovered, over medium/low heat for 10 minutes or until light, lime-infused syrup has formed.

3. Remove from heat, set aside to cool. Once cooled use a slotted spoon to remove lime zest from saucepan. Pour the syrup into a clean bottle and cork tightly. Store at room temperature until ready to use.

4. To serve mix in a ratio of: 1 part syrup, 3 parts water (or clubs soda), and 5 ice cubes per person. Server Chilled, and garnish with lime slices and/ or a spring of fresh mint.

variation:

Orange Syrup (sharbat'e Narenj): Follow the above recipe. Substitute 1 cup fresh orange juice for the fresh lime juice, and substitute the zest of one orange for the zest of one lime.

sour cherry syrup
sharbat'e albaloo

This blush sweet and sour drink is amazing in the summertime, in step 4 - I often use Club soda for a refreshing sparkling beverage, and garnish with a cherry! *makes 1 bottle of syrup*

Ingredients
2 cups water
2 cups sugar
¼ cup fresh lime juice
1 pound fresh sour cherries,
Wrapped in a bouquet garni
¼ teaspoon vanilla extract

Mixing:
Plain filter water, sparkling water,
or club soda
5 Ice cubes per person

garnish
Mint Leaves, cherries, or rosebuds
(optional)

Method

1. In a 4-quart porcelain or enamel saucepan place water and sugar, mix ingredients together until sugar has dissolved with a wooden spoon. Bring to a boil, and let simmer for 10 minutes. Stir occasionally with a wooden spoon.

2. Add the lime juice, cherry sachet, and cook, uncovered, over medium/low heat for 20 minutes or until light, cherry-infused syrup has formed.

3. Remove from heat, add vanilla extract, and set aside to cool. Once cooled, remove cherry sachet from saucepan. Pour the syrup into a clean bottle and cork tightly. Keep refrigerated, and use as needed.

4. To serve mix in a ratio of: 1 part syrup, 3 parts water (or clubs soda), and 5 ice cubes per person. Server Chilled, and garnish with mint leaves and/or rose buds.

Note: to make a bouquet garni place cherries in a large square peace of muslin, and tie all sides together with kitchen twine.

sweet and sour syrup
sharbat'e sekanjabin

This medieval drink was known by the ancient Greeks as oxymel, and was a favorite of the legendary shahs (kings) of Iran's past (the glory days). This syrup can be served as a beverage, or served as a dip alongside crisp Romaine leaves. *makes 1 bottle of syrup*

Ingredients
2 cups water
2 cups sugar
½ cup white vinegar
1 bunch fresh mint, washed, drained, and wrapped in a bouquet garni

Mixing:
Plain filter water, sparkling water, or club soda
5 Ice cubes per person

garnish
mint Leaves

Method

1. In a 4-quart porcelain or enamel saucepan place water and sugar, mix ingredients together until sugar has dissolved with a wooden spoon. Bring to a boil, and let simmer for 10 minutes. Stir occasionally with a wooden spoon.

2. Add the vinegar, mint sachet, and cook, uncovered over medium/low heat for 20 minutes or until light, mint-infused syrup has formed.

3. Remove from heat, and set aside to cool. Once cooled, remove mint sachet from saucepan. Pour the syrup into a clean bottle and cork tightly. Store at room temperature until ready to use.

4. To serve mix in a ratio of: 1 part syrup, 3 parts water (or clubs soda), and 5 ice cubes per person. Server chilled, and garnish with mint leaves.

Note: to make a bouquet garni place mint in a small square peace of muslin, and tie all sides together with kitchen twine.

variation:

Sweet & Sour syrup with cucumber (sharbat'e Khiar va Sekanjabin): Follow the above recipe, and in step 4 add thinly sliced Persian cucumbers. Serve chilled.

Sweet & Sour syrup with lettuce (sharbat'e Sekanjabin va kahu)
Follow the above recipe. However, in Step 4 pour syrup by its self in a bowl, serve along-side with hearts of romaine for dipping.

persian cure all elixir
arag'e tokhme sharbati

This is a treasured family secret known as a cure all elixir that is packed with omega 3's thanks to the chia seeds. I drink this four times a week as it aids in overall good health, along with weight management, and mental clarity. *serves 4*

Ingredients

2½ cups alkaline water
½ cup fresh lemon or lime juice
¼ cup Raw honey
½ bunch fresh mint, washed,
drained, finely chopped
1 tablespoon rosewater
2-3 teaspoons chia seeds
(Tokhme Sharbati)

garnish

Spring of fresh pint for garnish

Method

1. Place all ingredients in a large pitcher, and with a spoon mix all ingredients together. Refrigerate for at least 2 hour before serving.

2. Serve club with ice cubes, and garnish with a spring of mint.

rose milk
sheer golab

My mother would make this aromatic comforting bedtime drink for me every night as a child to ensure that I would have a wholesome sleep. This is an ancient Sufi remedy that is-said to be created by Rumi. serves 2

Ingredients
2 cups milk
2 tablespoons rose water
3 tablespoons raw honey
Pinch on Saffron

garnish
Threads of saffron

Method

1. In a medium saucepan place milk and gently warm milk over low heat. Add rose water and honey, and stir until honey is completely combined. Next stir in saffron, and simmer for 2 minutes uncovered.

2. Pour mixture into serving glasses, and garnish with threads of saffron.

desserts

shirini

Sweets are served all thought the day with warm tea. Moreover, A day would not be complete without platters of pastries and candy. Persian sweeties feature exotic flavors such as rose water, orange blossom water, and saffron. Persian pastries are greatly influence by French patisserie.

I find it very glamorous to bake I love how basic ingredients such as water, flour and eggs magically transform into delicious edible works of art. The most common desert found in a Persian home and at Persian celebrations is a tray adored with seasonal fresh cut fruits, also cold desserts such as ice cream are very popular after a heavy meal. Persian ice cream is creamy and rich, featuring exotic flavors such as rose water and orange blossom water.

saffron rice pudding
sholeh zard

Sholeh Zard is one of the loveliest puddings, rich and sweet and laced with cardamom and rose water. In my family we only make Sholeh Zard once a year as a Nazri (religious offering), and we distribute it to the poor and underprivileged. *serves 8*

Ingredients
1 cup rice
9 cups water
2½ cups granulated sugar
2 tablespoons butter
1 tablespoon cardamom
½ cup rose water
½ teaspoon ground saffron
(dissolved in 2 tablespoons hot water).

garnish
Ground cinnamon
Silvered Pistachios
Dried rose petals or hips

Method
1. Rinse rice with cold water until water runs clear, and drain.

2. In a medium-saucepan place drained rice and 9 cups of water, bring to a boil over high heat, and skim off any foam that rises. Once at a boil reduce heat to medium/low, cover, and cook for 40 minutes. Stir occasionally with a spoon.

3. Next gently stir in butter, sugar, cardamom, and saffron liquid to t he saucepan. Reduce heat to low and continue cooking for 20 minutes, or until the mixture is golden and creamy. Add rose water, stir, and cook for 5 minutes. Remove from heat.

4. Transfer pudding into individual ramekins, or large bowl.

5. Garnish with ground cinnamon, silvered pistachios, and dried rose petals, and cool in the refrigerator for 2 hours before serving.

ice in paradise
yakh dar behesht

Yakh Dar Behesht meaning ice in paradise, is a delicate custard usually prepared during the summer. When serving make-sure that the custard is well chilled before serving. *serves 8*

Ingredients
3 ¾ cups whole milk
1 cup rice flour
1 cup granulated sugar
1 tablespoon ground cardamom
¼ cup

garnish
Silvered pistachios
Dried rose petals

Method

1. In a medium-saucepan place milk, rice flour and sugar, bring to a boil over medium-low heat. Stir constantly with a wooden spoon to prevent the mixture from sticking to the saucepan (for about 12 minutes).

2. Lower the heat, and add rose water, and ground cardamom. Continue cooking, and stirring until a smooth custard is formed (about 10 minutes).

3. Remove from heat, pour custard into a silicone mold, or serving dish, and cool in the refrigerator for 2 hours before serving.

4. Transfer to serving dish, garnish with silvered pistachios, and rose petals.

saffron and rose ice cream
bastani'e akbar mashti

There is just something about homemade ice cream: it's the ultimate comfort food, or should I say ultimate comfort dessert. This is a light and aromatic ice cream with a subdued flavor of rose, weaved with lush chunks of frozen cream. serves 8

Ingredients
2 cups whole milk
3 cup heavy cream, divided
1¾ cups unsweetened evaporated milk
1 cup rose water
Pinch of saffron threads (grinded & dissolved in 2 tablespoons hot water)
½ cup granulated sugar
2 tablespoons pure ground sahlab/salep*
¼ cup silvered pistachios (optional)

garnish
Dried rose petals

Method
1. In a medium-saucepan place the milk, 2 cups cream, gently bring to a boil, reduce heat to low, an let simmer until the liquid is reduced by about a quarter (about 20-25 minutes). Stir occasionally with a wooden spoon to prevent liquid from boiling over. Add saffron liquid, ground sahlab, stir, and remove from heat. Set aside, and let stand for 15 minutes. Next strain the mixture trough a wire sieve into a large mixing bowl.
2. In a small saucepan place sugar, rose water, and combine over a low heat, stirring constantly with a wooden spoon until the sugar has dissolved (about 5 minutes). Let simmer for 5 minutes, or until a thin syrup forms. Remove from heat and let cool for 15 minutes.
3. Meanwhile, pour 1 cup heaving cream on a baking sheet lined with parchment paper, and freezer.
4. Pour the cooled sugar syrup mixture into the cream mixture, and stir until evenly incorporated. Refrigerate until well chilled, at least 4 hours, preferably overnight.
5. Pour the cooled milk mixture into a ice cream maker following the manufacturers' instructions. Remove cream from freezer, and break into little pieces.
6. Once the Ice cream if formed, add the broken cream pieces, and silvered pistachios to the ice cream machine, and let incorporate for 20 seconds.
7. Freeze ice cream for at least 4 hours, preferably overnight before serving.

pistachio and orange blossom ice cream ~ bastani'e pestehva bahar narenj

This delicate pale green ice cream has a subtle pistachio flavor, and smells heavenly thanks to the orange blossom water. This ice cream is a cinch to make, and makes a wonderful light finish to a heavy meal. serves 8

Ingredients
2 cups whole milk
2 cup heavy cream, divided
1¾ cups unsweetened evaporated milk
¼ cup orange blossom water
½ cup granulated sugar
½ cup silvered pistachios

Method
1. In a medium-saucepan place the milk, 2 cups cream, gently bring to a
1. Place pistachios, and sugar into a food processor, and pulse until the texture becomes a fine powder.

2. In a medium-saucepan place the pistachio mixture, milk, 2 cups cream, gently bring to a boil, reduce heat to low, and let simmer until the liquid is reduced by about a quarter (about 25-30 minutes). Stir occasionally with a wooden spoon to prevent liquid from boiling over. Add orange blossom water, evaporated milk, stir until evenly incorporated, and let simmer for 2 minutes.

3. Remove from heat. Set aside, and let stand for 15 minutes. Next strain the mixture trough a wire sieve into a large mixing bowl. Refrigerate until well chilled, at least 4 hours, preferably overnight.

4. Pour the cooled milk mixture into a ice cream maker following the manufacturers' instructions.

5. Freeze ice cream for at least 4 hours, preferably overnight before serving.

6. Serve ice cream in small bowls, or place ice cream in-between 2 round wafers to cake an ice cream sandwich.

carrot ice cream float
aab'e havij va bastani

I Just adore Aab'e Havij va Bastani it's my not-so-guilty indulgence. This carrot float is the Persian version of a root beer float. This float makes for a fun and delicious summer treat. Make sure to use fresh carrot juice it makes a world of a difference. *serves 2*

Ingredients
1 ½ Cup fresh carrot Juice
4 scoops rose water ice cream, vanilla ice cream or coconut milk ice cream

garnish
Pinch of ground cinnamon
Pinch of ground cardamom

Method
1. Place two tall freezer safe glasses in the freezer for 30 minutes.

2. Remove glasses from freezer, place two scoops of ice cream in each glass, and pour carrot juice into glasses. Garnish with a pinch of ground cinnamon, and ground cardamom.

iced rice noodle granita
faloodeh

Faloodeh is the world's first form of ice cream dating back to 400 BCE. Faloodeh is a mixture of shaved ice, rice noodles, rose water, sugar and fresh lime juice. Faloodeh is very popular throughout Iran, and there are different versions in different cities. The most famous Faloodeh is from Shiraz, to make Shirazi Faloodeh garnish your faloodeh atop with sour cherry preserves. serves 4-6

Ingredients
3 ounces very thin rice noodles
2 cups granulated sugar
2 cups water
½ cup fresh lime juice
1 ounce rose water

garnish
Fresh Lime wedges
Sour cherry Preserves (optional)

Method
1. In a Medium-saucepan place sugar, water, lime juice and combine over a low heat, stirring constantly with a wooden spoon until the sugar has dissolved (about 5 minutes). Let simmer for 5 more minutes, or until a thin syrup forms. Remove from heat and let cool for 15 minutes.
2. Place noodles in a heatproof bowl, cover with boiling water, and let stand for five minutes or until soft. Drain and rinse under cold water. With a kitchen scissors cut noodles into two-inch pieces.
3. Place drained noodles, and syrup into a medium metal mixing bowl, and combine. Place in the Freezer for 1 hour.
4. Remove bowl from the freezer, and rake with a fork to fluff the ice. Return bowl to freezer, and repeat this process twice more, or until desired consistency is reached.
5. Serve in individual serving bowls, with lime wedges, or a teaspoon of sour cherry Preserves.

variation:

Apple Granita (Faloodeh'e sib)
Peel and grate 5 green apples, Place apples into a medium metal mixing bowl. Add ½ cup lime juice, ¼ cup raw honey, and stir until evenly incorporated. Add 7 cups shaved ice, and mix ingredients together. Freezer for 15 minutes, remove bowl for freezer, and rake with a fork to fluff the ice. Serve in individual serving bowls, and garnish to your liking.

dense rose water confection halva

Persian Halva is a sweet honey-flavored dessert made from flour, and is an ancient recipe that dates back to the 18th century.
serves 4-6

Ingredients
1 cups all-purpose flour, sifted
1 cup water
1 cup granulated sugar
1 cup unsalted butter, melted
½ cup rose water
Pinch of saffron threads (grinded & dissolved in 2 tablespoons hot water)

Method
1. In a Medium-saucepan place sugar, water, and bring to boil over medium heat, stir constantly with a wooden spoon until the sugar has dissolved (about 5 minutes). Let simmer for 5 more minutes, or until a thin syrup forms. Remove from heat. Add saffron liquid, rose water and combined. Set aside.

3. In another medium-sized saucepan, place flour and toast over high heat while string constantly, until golden in color (no longer than 2 minutes). Reduce heat to medium, add the melted butter and cook for 7-10 minutes, still stirring constantly, until mixture forms into a smooth paste. Remove from heat.

4. Carefully add the syrup to the flour mixture, and mix vigorously for one minute, or until smooth. Then return the saucepan to the stove, over low heat, stirring continually until all the syrup has been absorbed into the mixture, and a smooth paste forms (approximately 4 minutes).

5. Remove from heat, and transfer halva to a serving plate, smooth and flatten the surface with the back of a spoon, and imprint half-moons into the surface use the side of a spoon. Or spread the halva onto a cleaned flat surface, and cut into shapes using a small cookie cutter.

6. Cover with plastic wrap, and refrigerate until well chilled.

decadent date cake
ranginak

Ranginak is a wonderful tasty dessert from the southern region of Iran. Ranginak has a soft chewy texture, and simply melts in your mouth. Ranginak is traditionally served with warm black tea.

serves 4-6

Ingredients

1 pond medjool dates
1 cup halved walnuts, or shelled pistachios
1 cups all-purpose flour, sifted
1 cup unsalted butter, melted
1 teaspoon ground cinnamon
1 teaspoon ground cardamom

garnish

¼ cup confectioner's sugar
pinch of ground cinnamon

Method

1. Carefully remove the pits from the dates, and insert a walnut half.

2. Arrange the stuffed-dates vertically one next to the other into a 9- inch pie dish.

3. In a medium-sized saucepan, place flour, melted butter, ground cinnamon, and ground cardamom. Cook over medium heat until golden in color, and mixture has a creamy consistency.

4. Carefully pour the mixture over the dates. Sprinkle evenly with confectioners' sugar, and cinnamon. Leave to cool at room temperature, for at least 4 hours before serving.

star cake
cake'e setareh

This is one of my favorite cakes. It's moist and dense, and filled with aromatic edible roses. Its truly delicious and supper impressive-looking; thanks to the fresh roses adorned at the top and bottom of the cake. The Farsi name for this cake is "Setareh" which means star and this cake is a ture star. *serves 4-6*

Ingredients For Cake

2 cups cake flower, (not self-rising)
2 tsp. baking powder
1/8 teaspoon salt
1 cup unsalted butter, softened
1 cup full-fat plain yogurt
1 teaspoon pure vanilla extract
1 ½ cup granulated sugar, sifted
6 egg whites (at room temperature)
1/4 cup fresh edible rose petals, diced, loosely-packed
3 teaspoon rose water

Ingredients For Frosting

12 oz cream cheese
(room temperature)
1½ cups heavy cream
1 cup confectioners' sugar, sifted
2 teaspoon rose water

garnish

1 cup fresh edible roses

Method

1. To prepare the frosting: in a medium mixing bowl place heavy cream, and whisk until medium to stiff peaks form (about 5 minutes). Set aside. In a separate mixing bowl place cream cheese, confectioners' sugar, rose water, and whip until smooth. Using a rubber spatula, Gradually fold the whipped cream into the cream cheese mixture. Set aside, and refrigerate until ready to use.

2. Adjust oven rack to the middle position, and preheat oven to 350° F. Line 3 6x2-inch round cake pans with parchment paper rounds, and butter pans.

3. In a medium bowl sift flour, baking powder, and salt together. Set aside. In the bowl of an stand mixer fitted with a paddle attachment, place butter, 1 cup sugar and mix together until light and fluffy, about 4 minutes. Add vanilla, place mixer on low, and gradually add flour mixture, alternating by adding yogurt, and continue beating until the batter is evenly incorporated (making sure not to over-mix the batter). Add ¼ cup rose petals, rose water and combine. Transfer batter to a large bowl, and set aside.

4. In the clean bowl of a stand mixer fitted with a whisk attachment, place egg whites, and beat on low speed until foamy. Next gradually add remaining 1/2 cup sugar, and beat on high speed until stiff, glossy peaks form (making sure not to over-beat the mixture). Gently/gradually fold the egg white mixture into the batter, while using a rubber spatula until combined.

5. Divide batter evenly between prepared pans, smoothing with an offset spatula. Bake until golden, about 30-35 minutes. Transfer pans to a cooling rack, and let cool completely for 1 hour. Invert cakes onto rack, peel off parchment, and reinvert cakes.

6. Using a serrated knife, trim tops of cake layers to make level. Place one layer on a serving plate, cut side up, and Place a large scoop of frosting and evenly spread over the top of the cake, gently place the second cake layer on top, cut side down, and frost. Next add the final layer of cake, cut side down. Spread entire cake with frosting, swirling to cover. Garnish cake atop with roses, and bottom of the cake with rose petals.

rose water roulade
rolette'e golab

This is a simple version of the classic French Roulade, that has been adapted into Persian cuisine. This enchanting cake is dusted with confectioners' sugar, and adored atop with cream and fresh strawberries. Trim the ends of this cake to reveal the swirls of cream filling. serves 4-6

Ingredients For Cake
5 organic eggs
1 cup granulated sugar
1 teaspoon vanilla extract
1 teaspoon backing powder
1½ cups cake flower, (not self-rising), sifted
¼ cup rose water, or orange blossom water
½ teaspoon ground cardamom

Ingredients For Frosting
1 cup heavy cream
2 tablespoons rosewater
¾ cup confectioners' sugar

garnish
¼ cup confectioners' sugar
4 strawberries
Leftover cream from filling

Method

1. To prepare the filling: in a medium mixing bowl place heavy cream, rose water, confectioners' sugar, and whip until soft to medium peaks form. Set aside, and refrigerate until ready to use.

2. Adjust oven rack to the middle position, and preheat oven to 400° F. Line one baking sheet with parchment paper, or a non-stick baking mat.

3. Using a stand mixer place eggs, beat eggs until fluffy, add vanilla, sugar, cardamom, and continue beating until the mixture is evenly incorporated (making sure not to over-mix the mixture).

4. Remove mixing bowl from the stand, and with a rubber spatula gently fold in sifted flour, and backing powder.

5. Next pour the batter directly onto the prepared baking sheet, spreading batter evenly with a rubber spatula. Bake for 15 minutes, or until lightly golden. Remove tray from the oven, place on a cooling rack, and let cool.

6. Once cooled turn the cake sheet out onto a clean flat surface dusted with confectioners' sugar, and remove parchment paper from the cake. Brush the cake with rose water, or orange blossom water with a pastry brush. Spread cream evenly onto the surface, using an offset spatula, leaving 1-inch border around all edges (make sure to leave some cream for the garnish). Tightly roll cake, by starting at 1 short side. Transfer seam side down onto a serving dish, garnish atop with confectioners' sugar, and 4 dollops of cream. Next place strawberries on top of cream dollops. Refrigerate for at least 1 hour before serving.

Note: Recipes are listed in Farsi and English in alphabetial order. A bracketed pink (V) indicates a vegetarian recipe.

-A-
Aab'e Havij Va Bastani, 148 (V)
Abgush, 71
Addas Polo, 104
Advieh-ye khoresh, 34 (V)
Advieh-ye Polow, 34 (V)
Advieh-ye kabob, 33
Albaloo Polo, 96 (V)
Apple Granita, 149 (V)
Araq'e Tokhme Sharbati, 14 (V)
Aromatic Herb Rice, 100 (V)
Aromatic Herb Salad, 53
Aromatic Herb Love Stew, 80
Ashapzi Ba Zaferan, 37 (V)
Ash'e Anar, 68
Ash'e Reshteh, 69
Assyrian Curry Stew, 83

-B-
Baked Saffron Yogurt Rice
with Chicken, 103
Baqhala Polo, 98 (V)
Barbari Bread, 61 (V)
Barberry Saffron Rice, 97 (V)
Bastani'e Akbar Mashti, 146 (V)
Bastani'e Pesteh Va
Bahar Narenj, 147 (V)
Borani'e labe, 45 (V)
Bread, 57-65

-C-
Cafe Glace, 134 (V)
Cake'e Setareh, 152 (V)
Carrot Ice Cream float, 148 (V)
Chai, 132 (V)
Celery Stew, 88
Chelo, 92 (V)
Chelo Kabob, 107
Chicken Braised with yogurt
and olives, 116
Chicken Broth, 38
Chicken Fillet Kabob, 113
Chicken Kabob, 114
Chickpea Patties with Sweet &
Sour Sauce, 51
Creamy Turkey Porridge with
Cinnamon, 75

-D-
Decadent Date Cake, 151 (V)
Dense Rose Water Confection,
150 (V)
Dolmeh'ye Barg'e Angur, 49 (V)
Dolmeh'ye Beh, 111
Dolmeh'ye Kalam 112
Doogh, 135 (V)

-E-
Eggplant And Egg Spread, 46 (V)
Eggplant Stew, 85
Estamboli Polo, 88

-F-
Faloodeh, 149 (V)
Faloodeh'e Sib, 149 (V)
Fava Bean & Dill Rice, 98 (V)
Feta & Egg Dip, 47 (V)
Fillet Kabob, 107
Fresh Herb Frittata, 56 (V)

-G-
Ghalieh Mahi, 89
Gol'e Mohammadi Polo, 101 (V)
Green Bean Rice, 99
Green Bean Stew, 86
Ground Meat Kabob, 108

-H-
Haleem, 75
Halibut Braised in Pomegranate
and orange juice, 119
Halva, 150 (V)
Herbs, 26-27
Herb Meatballs, 50
Homemade Butter, 38 (V)

-I-
Iced Coffee, 134 (V)
Ice In Paradise, 145 (V)
Iced Rice Noodle Granita, 149 (V)
Ingredients, 24-34

-J-

Javaher Polo, 95-96 (V)
Jeweled Rice, 95-96 (V)
Joojeh Kabab, 114

-K-

Kabab'e Barg, 107
Kabab'e Koobideh, 108
Kabab'e, 117
Kabab'e Morgh'e Barg, 113
Khoresh'e Albalo, 87
Khoresh'e Bedemjane, 85
khoresh'e Beh, 79
Khoresh'e Cari, 83
khoresh'e Esfenaj'o Alu Zard, 78
Khoresh'e Fesenjan, 81
khoresh'e Geymeh, 82
Khoresh'e Gormeh Sabzi, 80
Khoresh'e Hulu, 79
Khoresh'e Karafs, 88
Khoresh'e Lubia, 86
Khoresh'e Narengi, 84
Khoresh'e Rivas, 88
Kateh, 102 (V)
Koofteh Sabzi, 50
Koofteh Tabrizi, 110
Kuku'y Sabzi, 56 (V)

-L-

Lavash Flat Beard, 59 (V)
Lavash Potato Turnover, 52
Lime Syrup, 137
Lubia Polo, 99 (V)

-M-

Mahi Ba Ab'e Miveh, 119
Mahi'e Shekampor, 118
Mast , 39 (V)
Mast-e Kisseh, 39 (V)
Mast'o Khiar, 44 (V)
Mezzehs, 42-56
Mirza Ghasem, 46 (V)
Mixed Pickled Vegetables, 125 (V)
Moraba'ye Albalu, 123 (V)
Moraba'ye Beh, 122 (V)
Moraba'ye Gol'e Sorkh, 124 (V)
Morgh'e Mast Ba Zaytoon, 116
Morgh'e Shekampor, 115

-N-

Nan'e Barbari, 61 (V)
Nan'e Ghandi, 64 (V)
Nan'e Lavash, 59 (V)
Nan'e Pita, 63 (V)
Nan'e Taftoon, 60 (V)
Nan'e Sangak, 62 (V)
Noodle Soup, 69 (V)

-O-

Orange Syrup, 137 (V)

-P-

Panir Bereshteh, 47 (V)
Peach Stew, 79
Persian Chicken Salad, 54
Persian Cure All Elixir, 140, (V)
Persian Holidays & Customs, 14-23
Persian Kabob Spice Mix, 33
Persian Matzo ball Soup
Persian Stew Spice Mix, 34 (V)
Persian Sticky Rice, 102 (V)
Persian Rice Spice Mix, 34 (V)
Persian Coffee, 133 (V)
Persian Tea, 132 (V)
Pickled Cherries, 127 (V)
Pickled Garlic, 128 (V)
Pickled Grapes, 126 (V)
Pickled Pistachios, 129 (V)
Pistachio & Orange Blossom Ice Cream, 147 (V)
Pita Bread, 63 (V)
Pomegranate And Walnut Stew, 81
Pomegranate Marinated Olives, 48 (V)
Pomegranate Molasse, 40 (V)
Pomegranate Soup, 68

-Q-

Qahveh, 133
Quince Stew, 79
Quince Preserves, 112 (V)

-R-

Ranginak, 151 (V)
Red Rice With Fillet Mignon, 99
Rice, 30-31, 90-104
Rice with brown lentils, raisins
& dates, 104 (V)
Rhubarb & Mint Stew, 88
Roasted Chicken stuffed
with apricots, & prunes, 115
Rolette'e Golab, 153 (V)
Rose Bud Rice, 101 (V)
Rose Milk, 141 (V)
Rose Petal Preserves, 124 (V)
Rose Water Drink, 136 (V)
Rose Water Roulade, 153 (V)

-S-

Sabzi Polo, 100
Sabzi Khordan, 53 (V)
Saffron And Rose Ice Cream, 146 (V)
Saffron Cream of Rice Soup, 73
Saffron Emulsion, 37 (V)
Saffron Ghe, 41 (V)
Saffron Rice Pudding, 144 (V)
Saffron Steamed Rice, 92 (V)
Salad'e Olivieh, 54
Salad'e Shiraz, 55 (V)
Salmon Kabob, 117
Samboseh , 52
Sangak Bread, 62 (V)
Shami, 51
Sharbat'e Albalo, 138 (V)
Sharbat'e Golab,136 (V)
Sharbat'e Limo, 137 (V)
Sharbat'e Narenj, 137 (V)
Sharbat'e Khiar Va Sekanjabin, 139 (V)
Sharbat'e Sekanjabi, 139 (V)
Sheer Golab, 141 (V)
Shirin Polo, 95 (V)
Sholeh Zard, 144 (V)
Soup'e Berenji, 73 (V)
Soup'e Aroosi, 70
Soup'e Gojeh Farangi, 72 (V)
Soups, 66-75
Sour Cherry Preserves, 123 (V)
Sour Cherry Rice, 96
Sour Cherry Stew, 87
Sour Cherry Syrup, 138 (V)
Spicy Tamarind Fish Stew, 89

Spinach & Golden Plum Stew, 78
Star Cake, 152 (V)
Stews, 76-89
Stuffed Cabbage Leaves, 112
Stuffed Grape Leaves, 49 (V)
Stuffed Quince, 111
Sweet & Sour Syrup, 139 (V)
Sweet & Sour Syrup with cucum-
ber, 139 (V)
Sweet Milk Rice, 101 (V)
Sweet Rose Flat Bread, 64 (V)
Sweet Saffron Rice, 95 (V)

-T-

Tabriz Meatballs, 110
Tachin-e Morgh, 103
Tadig, 92-23
Taftoon Flat Bread, 60 (V)
Tamarind Infused Stuffed Red
Sanpper, 118
Tangerine Chicken Stew, 84
Tas Kabab, 109
Tender Beef Braised with
Cinnamon & Prunes, 109
Tender Lamb With pulses Soup,
71
Tomato & Cucumber Salad, 55 (V)
Tomato Soup, 72 (V)
Torshi'ye Angoor, 126 (V)
Torshi'ye Gilas, 127 (V)
Torshi'e Makhlut, 125 (V)
Torshi'ye Pesteh, 129 (V)
Torshi'ye Seer, 128 (V)

-U-

Unani, 10-13

-V-

Vegetable Broth, 38 (V)

-W-

Wedding Soup, 70

-Y-
Yellow Split Pea & Potato Stew, 82
Yakh Dar Behesht, 145 (V)
Yogurt, 39 (V)
Yogurt & cucumber dip, 44 (V)
Yogurt & beetroot dip, 45 (V)
Yogurt Soda, 135 (V)

-Z-
Zeytoon Parvardeh, 48 (V)
Zereshk Polo, 97

Bibliography

Null, Gary. *The Complete Guide to Health and Nutrition*. New York: Dell, 1984
Ahmad, Jamil. *Ahmad Unani: The Science of Graeco Arabic Medicine*. Indian: Roli Books Pvt Ltd, 1998
Ukers, William H. *The Romance of Tea*. Alfred A. Knopf. New York: 1936.
Cousi, Jean Pierre. *Food is Medicine*. Duncan Baird. London: 2001.

Notes:

www.ingramcontent.com/pod-product-compliance
Lightning Source LLC
Chambersburg PA
CBHW040939100426
42812CB00016B/2628